HOW TO BECOME INSPIRED AND INSPIRATIONAL

HOW TO BECOME INSPIRED AND INSPIRATIONAL

The Importance of Nurturing Talent

Steve Sonntag

ROWMAN & LITTLEFIELD
Lanham • Boulder • New York • London

Published by Rowman & Littlefield
An imprint of The Rowman & Littlefield Publishing Group, Inc.
4501 Forbes Boulevard, Suite 200, Lanham, Maryland 20706
https://rowman.com

Unit A, Whitacre Mews, 26-34 Stannary Street, London SE11 4AB, United Kingdom

Copyright © 2019 by Steve Sonntag

All rights reserved. No part of this book may be reproduced in any form or by any electronic or mechanical means, including information storage and retrieval systems, without written permission from the publisher, except by a reviewer who may quote passages in a review.

British Library Cataloguing in Publication Information Available

Library of Congress Cataloging-in-Publication Data Available

ISBN 978-1-4758-4616-4 (cloth : alk. paper)
ISBN 978-1-4758-4617-1 (pbk. : alk. paper)
ISBN 978-1-4758-4618-8 (electronic)

When there is community, there is hope.
　　—Steve Sonntag

CONTENTS

Acknowledgments	ix
Introduction	1

I: THE *TALENTED* ELEMENTS OF YOUR LIFE
1 The Time and the Space to Be Talented	5
2 Your Ability to Be Talented	17
3 The Ramifications and the Purpose of Your Talent	41

II: THE *EMOTIONAL* ELEMENTS OF YOUR LIFE
4 Your Family History	51
5 Your Emotional Tides Can Influence Your Life Perspective	61

III: THE *COMMUNITY* ELEMENTS OF YOUR LIFE
6 Your Attitude and Your Education	69
7 Your Educational Life	77
8 Acceptance	97
9 Being Selfish vs. Self-full	105
10 Pride and the Art of Humility	109
11 The Gratitude Attitude	113
12 Our Children Are Our Future!	119
Bibliography	123
About the Author	125

ACKNOWLEDGMENTS

I wish to dedicate *How to Become Inspired and Inspirational: The Importance of Nurturing Talent* to my parents, Lewis L. Sonntag and Natalie R. Sonntag; to the rest of my relatives; and especially to my maternal grandmother, Rebecca Yaspan, who literally saved my life, gave me personal attention and love, and really was my mentor who originally inspired me to teach.

During my school years, my school counselor, Mr. Osegueda; my Spanish teachers, Mr. Harvey, Mrs. Cannon, and Dr. Galán; and the international program director, Dr. Lantos, were particularly helpful and encouraging. It was because of their sincerity to students and their dedication to the school community that I also chose to become a teacher. Indeed, they were great role models for others as well for myself.

My personal friends Janice Lee, the Ballew family, Woody Brown, Miklos Fejer, Mike Forman, Arlene Krauss, Thu Lam, Leo and Aziza Mara, Michelle and Giovanna Mercurio, Christian Mitchell, Jordan Mitchell, the O'Leary family, the Shalom-Nautico Community, Karen Steves-Ott, Adele Stinson, and Debbie Sugarman are very loving and very supportive and have helped me both personally and professionally. Jerry Hackett and his philosophy of being self-full in order to become better personally helped me and he has unfortunately passed.

My professional friends Dr. Edward Brasmer, Marcia Chapman, Carol De Sá Campos, Mindie Dolson, Denise Elling, Sarah Fox, Jeff Gaines, Terri Godinez, Barbara Henry, Bill Jones, Joe Mora, Nina Norton, Bonna Purdy, and Jim Stoker have been exceptionally wonderful role models for so many people as well as for myself.

I also extend my professional acknowledgment to Bertram Linder, the educational literary agent who guided me with my previous books for teachers and for families and who has unfortunately passed.

Along with all of my former students and parents from Manteca High School in Manteca, California, I have had the pleasure of working with other students and their parents from Connecting Waters Charter School based out of Modesto, California, and with adults who are also very inspirational, intelligent, and humble. Those particular people have been Allie, Alyssa, Annie, Beau, Connor, David, Davis, Derek, Dylan, Erin, Katie, Laura, Lauren, Lexy, Lia, Margaret, Matthew, Miya, Patrick, Salima, Sarah, Shane, Sofia, Tiffany, and Yasmin.

Jenna is a unique young lady whose perspective about life is very positive, and she is very humble. Her attitude and her personality are truly allowing her to achieve all of her goals in her life while being an outstanding role model for her family, friends, and everyone else whom she encounters.

To all of you whom I honor in this acknowledgment, thank you for being you. I admire all of you immensely.

INTRODUCTION

When there is community, there is hope. We are able to live to our potential. We can feel happier. We can become inspired by what is going on around us. We can become inspirational for others around us. On the other hand, there can be stumbling blocks called setbacks and mistakes in this road of life that we are all traveling.

So, how do we shift from pleasing others first and foremost to fulfilling our own needs? It is by doing our best to prioritize our own needs and then reaching out to others as needed while respectfully humbling ourselves to their knowledge and to their insight. This book will allow you to juggle the world around you with your own sense of self while balancing a private life.

Our professional lives have become so goal driven on account of our global society. We are always in competition locally, nationally, and globally in order to gain a positive reputation and money. We have to be the best qualified and to interview exceptionally well in order to be considered for any job that is available.

Our jobs become so reliant on how well we can develop the best, the most innovative products and our ability to attract customers on a regular basis. It means putting a lot of elbow grease into promoting the products by means of the media. It means following through with potential customers in order to see if they are interested in the products. So, our ability to have a creative talent can be a great resource for ourselves in terms of our professions.

Otherwise, there is always that chance we may be laid off or fired due to the company's inability to have made any kind of profit or our inability to "bring in the business." Under those circumstances, it can be very disheartening, no matter how logical we may perceive this departure from the job.

We need a time-out from all of the distractions that surround us on a daily basis. We need our personal space. We need to relax our brains so that we can reenergize ourselves so that we can regain and solidify our uniqueness. This can be done by allowing ourselves to become more creative in any number of ways by ourselves, without anyone being critical of what we are doing. In fact, it really does not matter what others think when we do something that is fulfilling for ourselves while we learn how to gently and respectfully balance our personal goals with family time and professional obligations.

How to Become Inspired and Inspirational: The Importance of Nurturing Talent can help you to focus on your given talent or your ability to realize it and the resources that are available for you in order to learn, and ultimately to provide for your community, namely your family, your job, and your friends. It is a realistic guide, because continuous success is not always possible due to having to learn from one's mistakes. In turn, they can provide opportunities to generate success.

This book is broken into three parts to consider in order to improve your life: the *Talented* Elements of Your Life, the *Emotional* Elements of Your Life, and the *Community* Elements of Your Life. Each of these parts will give you validation of life now and will inspire you to evolve yourself and to have joy in your life and quite possibly to become an inspiration for others around you both personally and professionally.

I

The *Talented* Elements of Your Life

I

THE TIME AND THE SPACE TO BE TALENTED

Your life can be inundated with responsibilities from the time you wake up to the time you go to bed. You need time to get yourself ready to meet your daily responsibilities. You need to mentally prepare yourself for whatever demands are made on your life. For example, there is breakfast to prepare in order to energize yourself and possibly others in your dwelling for the start of everyone's day, and there is the time to be devoted to working, which truly can become very energizing and perhaps even very stressful, based on the kind of job you have.

When work is completed at the end of the day, there may be other responsibilities that need to be taken care of, based on whether you are single or married and whether you have a family. If you have a significant other and/or children, you probably will try to have quality time with them. If you have children involved in sports or music lessons, you may need to transport them to different places. You may have household things to take care of, and if you are required to do office work at home due to not completing it at work, those kinds of obligations can interfere with your quality time for yourself and with others.

You may try to devote time to your friends. You may belong to a church or to a club that may want you to fulfill certain goals with them and for them. You may wish to maintain a healthy regimen of exercise as much as possible for at least thirty minutes each weekday. You may want to explore the internet for pleasure and/or for business purposes by means of social networking and general searches. Indeed, you may feel so exhausted by the time you have finished with your daily responsibilities that you may not want to do anything whatsoever, except for eating, cleaning up, and watching some television, for example.

During the weekends, you may spread yourself thin with different aspects of your life. You still may need to complete certain responsibilities for your job. There probably will be laundry to wash. There probably will be bills to be taken care of. There probably will be food and clothes shopping to be done. If you have children, you may have events that you wish to attend in order to support them. There probably will be family celebrations, such as birthdays, anniversaries, parties, and annual events, including Thanksgiving and religious holidays.

You may try to squeeze in some recreation, like going to the movies, watching recorded programs that are too late during the workweek, and reading a book, for example. Indeed, your supposed free time can be very full even during the weekend.

When extended weekends are available, you may experience exhaustion due to having to work more intensely during your workdays. You may wish to make plans to rest, but it may be challenging to do so when you have so much on your mind due to your professional responsibilities. You may wish to remain at home so that you may work on certain house projects. You may make plans to travel and feel tired, thus wondering how time has flown by so quickly with Monday being the next day.

Even if you have a so-called normal schedule as described above, when there are weddings, parties, emergencies, and funerals to attend, this creates a change in your routine and different emotions. While positive events such as weddings and parties can be fun, emergencies and funerals can create a major amount of sad emotions that you would prefer not to experience, although you know that all of these kinds of events are normal in your life.

Here is a noteworthy example for your consideration. There were five teachers who were born and raised in Spain. They heard about a California school district that was hiring teachers from out of the country. They heard they could earn 100 percent more in salary. Thus, they were very excited and chose to apply. They eventually were hired and flew to California.

While they indeed earned 100 percent more in their salary, they had 100 percent more responsibilities. Being young Spaniards, they were hoping to do about the same amount of work as they had been doing and to have a lot of free time as in Spain; however, quite the opposite was true. They only had thirty minutes each day for their lunch break. They did have their free time, but not as much as they were accustomed to. So, four of five of them returned to Spain after teaching only one year, and the fifth one returned several years later.

The point to be learned from the above example of the Spaniards is that they had determined that life for them is not all work. We as a society can learn from them. While we need to work in order to have the comforts that we wish to have and to be involved with, there needs to be more of an opportunity to enjoy our lives without the constant exposure and stress of work-related issues.

In order to feel more invigorated and to evolve more of your own talented self, those periods of time called weeknights, weekends, and vacations deserve to be used for escaping from your normal routines and your normal responsibilities.

A school psychologist once said that people normally take time off from work when they are physically sick. So, why not take a day off to take care of yourself so that you don't become sick, especially when you may feel you are on the verge of becoming sick? So, why not take a day off to alleviate some of or a lot of your stress and totally relax around your home without making any phone calls, without involving yourself with your technological devices, without having any responsibilities whatsoever, and just read, watch television, or sleep for part or all of the day? This is a great way to recharge yourself.

This makes a lot of sense, although you may feel guilty for taking a mental health day to relax when you typically take time off from work only for illness or for emergencies of one form or another, for example. On the other hand, it is very well possible that you will feel healthier and will be able to fulfill your job responsibilities with that much more efficiency and perhaps even with more creativity when you decide to take a day off during the workweek.

Let's look at your daily responsibilities from a different point of view. Granted, you need to devote a lot of time and a lot of energy involving yourself in your professional responsibilities, which can allow you to have a more personal, more fulfilling life. Nevertheless, all work and no play is just as bad as all play and no work. When too much energy is focused on work, your mind can just be too involved in it. When it is time to relax and to sleep, it is very conceivable that it will be a challenge for you to fall asleep right away due to having been so heavily involved in your job during the waking hours.

When too much time is devoted to playing, this is not being realistic. In fact, it is living irrationally when there are living expenses to pay in order to survive or, even better yet, to thrive. Eventually, no more money will be available, and the hard case of reality will set in. Then, any job will be preferable to none in order to earn money for expenses.

When you focus more time and more energy on your profession, on your family, or on your friends, rather than having a balance for all of them, there will be an imbalance, which is unhealthy for yourself and for others around you.

Let's take this possible example: You are married. Your significant other devotes many countless hours to his work, leaving early in the morning and returning around dinnertime. After dinner, he sits in front of the computer for several hours. He then feels so tired that he decides to go to bed.

Would you like to be the spouse in such a situation? It would be difficult to deal with such a hardworking individual that devotes so much time and concentrates with so much effort. The significant other could rationalize these actions, saying that it is to have the luxuries of life; however, if such a situation were continuous, it is only natural that there would be a major strain in the family dynamics, maybe even drastically resulting in a separation or a divorce, unless the hardworking individual realizes how important having a personal life is and also to have a realistic balance of the work world and family living.

Here is another thought for your consideration. When you give so much of yourself that you feel completely drained, that is unhealthy and so very unkind to yourself. You can become completely exhausted and so frustrated that it is very well possible that you will become very resentful while others seemingly are doing nothing.

When you seemingly become oblivious of others, you are draining others of their value. You become rather selfish while others will come to the realization that you are just overwhelming them with your constant needs without ever once considering that others have their needs to be fulfilled as well. You and they need each other's companionship instead of just dwelling under the same roof.

Let's look at both giving and taking. When you are the kind of person who genuinely cares about others and is helpful, you tend to give freely of yourself to others. They feel good about what you do, although they may feel rather embarrassed or shy about it due to the generosity of your actions toward them; however, you feel really happy to have helped.

When you are always asking for something, people will tend to judge you as being too much of a needy person and a taker. Consequently, people will regard you as being selfish and will look the other way or eventually deny your request for whatever is needed.

When you have the ability to balance time for your profession, for your family, and for your friends, you know how to give as well as to receive. You will be able to give what you can, and you will be able to willingly accept what others offer to you. You can definitely feel self-full. You will feel happy. Others will enjoy your presence. Indeed, moderation is exceptionally important to be practiced, although this can be easily said while being rather difficult to exercise.

If and when there are demands that require you to devote more time to your profession or more time to your family or friends during your free time, it is very important to give quality time to whatever or whoever needs attention and then to create more personal time for yourself.

When you begin to allow yourself to potentially flourish creatively and to evolve your natural talents, you are giving yourself free time while realizing there are times that it is important to give to others as well. In a manner of speaking, this is your "brain vacation," your ability to relax your brain. By the way, this author uses the word *vacation* as an acronym, standing for "void all chaos and take in outstanding nature." Indeed, voiding yourself even temporarily can allow you to give yourself your personal space, your personal boundary, in order to fulfill something you wish to do or to ponder the possibilities freely without distractions.

Prior to delving into the theme of your talent when you allow it to evolve, let's define some terms. According to the World Book Dictionary, talent is "a special natural ability." Thus, your talent is totally ingrained within yourself. It may be enclosed in your mind in which there are creative glimmers or lights of ideas. It may come in the form of hunches, dreams, daydreams, or sudden flashes of ideas due to what you see or hear, all of which can be the result of your naturally designed talent.

When you allow yourself to be distracted by technological devices, your talent can be tarnished. You can become obsessed with or even addicted to them, because you wish to connect with people on social media and/or to play games by yourself and/or with others. In turn, it is almost like you are mentally blocking that part of you that deserves to blossom. Of course, if you are using a technological device in order to develop your talent, that is a different story.

According to the World Book Dictionary, creativity is "the act of being inventive and productive." Thus, upon acknowledging your talent, the formation of these ideas is the creative process. Your action is based on this talent that may or may not be successful, depending on how you feel about your project, the details of your project, and if or when you intend to pursue this idea for public use.

So, how do you develop the appropriate balance of being responsible to your work, being available for family and friends, and still allowing yourself time for your talent and your creativity to begin and to continuously flourish?

In psychological terms, boundaries are essential in order to develop your time and your space. It means saying to yourself and to others that you are important to your beautiful self and to your human becoming. You deserve and are entitled to your free time and your free space in order to be able to develop and to evolve without any responsibilities from anyone in your family for a while.

Of course, this cannot normally be done at work, seeing that you are required to be attentive to what you are supposed to be doing in order to be paid. Nevertheless, if your profession is to use your talent and your creativity on a regular basis, it can then be easy to be tuned into your happiness both for work and for home.

At home, that may mean saying to yourself and to others that a specific time period of the day needs to be yours for your own creativity, and everyone who has become reliant upon you needs to be respectful of your time and your space. That may mean working on something that you enjoy.

It is also suggested to silence or shut off your smartphone and perhaps even any other technological device so that you are not distracted whatsoever, unless your technological device will help you with your own personal project. If you do need a technological device such as a tablet, please make sure that it does not have a phone with it. If it does, please be sure to put it on silent and to put the cover on it so that you will not be distracted.

If there is a landline phone in the room, it is best to take it out of the room so that it does not interfere with what you are doing, if anyone calls your home.

This time needs to be consistent each day, the time in which you can be alert enough to focus on whatever your project may consist of. You need to form a habit that can be cultivated to not only keep your sanity despite the hectic world around you, but also to quite possibly develop a profitable venture for you, if you so desire. It will also show others that you respect yourself by doing something without any form of interference for the amount of time you deem desirable for yourself. You may even begin to look forward to this precious time just for yourself, especially after devoting so much time and so much energy to other people at your job and at home.

Your personal space is essential to maintain. That may mean shifting some things in your home to provide your own area for your own creative work. Even if it is a part of a room, it is your personal space. If it turns out to be a room that had been used for other things but that no longer is the case, it can become your personal space. Family members need to understand that just as their things are precious to them, your things need to be untouched, because they belong to you. It may take some time to accomplish; however, you are worth it.

If it is a part of the room that others in your home need, it is important to mention to them that you need your time and your space. If they need anything from that part of the room, it is a good idea to ask them to get those items before you begin. Otherwise, they need to wait until you are finished. Your ability to concentrate is really very important to constantly maintain.

If there is no possibility to acquire enough space for yourself and for your personal projects, if weather permits, you may wish to go to a place outside your home to work on your own project. If you are an artist, maybe there is a patio just outside in your backyard. In this way, you are outside and away from any distractions from your home, like anyone who lives with you and any noise from televisions, for example.

If it would be too noisy both inside and outside your home, you could venture to a scenic area to stay there for a while to draw, like before and/or after work. If staying there is not a possibility, how about taking the right photo so that you can take it home? Of course, you can take more than one photo so that you can draw an assortment of paintings or have them as your wallpaper on your computer screen, if you are doing computer work.

If your time is precious and limited, you may wish to do a Google search of different kinds of scenes and to develop your own paintings from what you have researched. The only drawback of doing such a search is that there is something to be said about being at the place itself. You can see everything around you. You can hear everything around you. You can smell everything around you. In contrast to doing such a search, you will thus be able to immerse yourself in the whole setting, which can allow you to have a better perspective of what you are working on.

If you draw or if you photograph places, you may wish to organize a portfolio and explore the options of having them published in a magazine.

Another possible place to gain your solitude is inside a library. In this way, you may draw, write, or just simply think, all of which are extremely important for the creative portion of your life. If the library has rooms that can be reserved and if you wish to reserve one, it is best to do so in order to have your complete space and your solitude for the allotted time.

Even if you do not create something, it is always great to simply relax completely in your favorite chair or in your bed, because besides having time to relax in order to develop your talent and your creativity, it is also important for you to relax without always having to generate ideas and things.

When completely relaxing and by working on creative projects not related to your profession, you are actually nurturing your own self and helping yourself for your profession so that you may be that much more efficient. A relaxed state of being is essential for yourself and for others around you, because you will feel calmer about yourself, about what you are doing, and about others with whom you associate. In turn, others may feel your calmness, and they too may feel more relaxed.

Even while exercising, this can be a great time to let your mind wander and to develop those talents that you wish to pursue. There is something rather invigorating about moving your body that can help your mind not only focus on these exercising motions, but also create inspirational thoughts for yourself. In order to transfer your mind into this creative state, it is suggested to have as few distractions—such as an iPod, a smartphone, and a television—as possible.

Taking a shower or a bath in the morning and/or at night can be your personal time and your personal space as well. When you feel the water and the soap surrounding yourself, you will cleanse your body, and you may even place yourself into some form of meditative state. It is very well possible to suddenly have a flash of an idea that you may not have thought of previously.

Having a spa treatment or getting a massage in which you allow yourself to focus on yourself while someone helps you can be such an enjoyable, relaxing experience, with the great side benefit being that you can cleanse yourself of stress and thus allow yourself to focus on your talent. It is very well possible that you may have a glimmer of an idea, which ultimately may result in something of value to yourself and quite possibly for others.

It is amazing that when you allow your mind to drift off, there is a very good tendency to develop your ideas, something seemingly whimsical and even inspirational. Along with your ideas being able to surge, if there are any personal or professional issues or challenges that are pressing, it is possible for you to determine specific solutions to those as well.

Traveling to work can allow the necessary creativity to emerge. If you take public transportation or if you are driven in a carpool, this portion of your day can become a great time to explore your creativity; your mind can wander as you write down ideas or draw some sketches using a notepad, a clipboard with blank paper, your laptop, or any other technological device you may have. If you prefer to simply gaze outside, you may just be able to determine some random, unique ideas that evolve into solutions of issues or allow yourself to develop an idea that may lead to something very helpful and very inspirational.

If you customarily drive to work, if there are alternate routes that can be taken without being an excessive amount of extra time, please consider taking them, because you are allowing yourself the opportunity to think differently based on the routes that you decide to take. When you choose to think differently, you may be able to create many more possibilities in order to resolve challenges and to have moments of enlightenment that will serve you and others very well.

Daydreaming while having some free time can generate an inspirational idea for yourself. You may be working on something entirely different when you suddenly determine a solution to a problem or have an important glimpse of a possible idea. Of course, it is inappropriate and, in fact, dangerous to daydream if you are using any potentially dangerous mechanical equipment, such as a car, or are engaged in any other activity that requires your complete attention. Under these circumstances, you need to concentrate on what you are doing for the sake of the safety of others and of yourself.

When doing work, an idea may suddenly appear in your mind, but please refocus on your work in order to complete the tasks at hand for your safety and anyone else around you. Then, when appropriate, note your idea on paper or in your smartphone so that you will remember it, refer to it, and develop it in more detail later on.

While it may seem strange, you can be productive and useful even when you are asleep. Your dreams or visions can become your gateway to your talent and to your creativity. In fact, it is advisable to have a notepad next to your bed to jot down your dreams or visions, because you may vividly or partially remember them when you have awakened. Another reason for the notepad next to your bed is that as your morning develops, you are more apt to begin focusing on what needs to be accomplished for your daily responsibilities, thus lessening the chances of remembering any specifics of your visions.

By jotting down specific words and/or by sketching those things that you recall, you are reminding yourself about those things you may wish to act upon, which may result in changing your plan for your project. Then, it is very well possible that you can remember more of what you had been dreaming, and you may very well expand and perfect these visions, thus making you feel that much more fulfilled and happy.

Your emotions and your moods can be either very helpful or very detrimental. If you are happy, more creativity can be the end product. You can feel happy, positive, energetic, and filled with inspirational ideas.

Should you be in a lethargic mood, a care-less mood, or feeling sad, it might be rather difficult to develop any ideas whatsoever, because you could be so immersed in your emotions and with whatever seems to be preoccupying yourself at that time.

Since everyone is different, it is possible that you may be able to live with depression while still having the ability to create something unique, similar to Edgar Allan Poe of the United States and Gustavo Adolfo Bécquer of Spain, nineteenth-century writers who both experienced depression but had an enormous, beautiful ability to create literature.

As a result, it is important to experience all kinds of emotions and moods in terms of your creative talent so that you can learn from them and possibly use them. It can be very refreshing for you personally, for your personal relationships, for your professional relationships, as well as for your professional work. In fact, you may even be honored for your unique ways of thinking.

It really becomes a winning situation for yourself when you allow yourself to have the time and the space for your personal fulfillment. You will feel relaxed. You can become that much more inspired about life. People around you will have the same benefits. When everyone is in agreement as to quality time with one another, all of you will have quality relationships along with quality time for your creative pursuits.

As for the project you personally wish to pursue, it is suggested that you ponder the possibilities as to what you wish to develop and to take as long as you wish to ponder. After all, this is your own special project, and no one is applying pressure to you.

Once you have determined what you wish to develop, getting whatever is needed is the next best step, whether you have the materials in your home or need to buy the materials. If the costs need to be revised so that you can develop your project, so be it. The idea is that you will have most of the materials possible so that you can focus your attention on what you wish to do.

It is from this point that your mind, your talent, and your creativity will have a goal. You may remain steadfast in your determination to complete the project as you first designed it. You may decide, as you develop your project, that you wish to make changes that may result in something similar to what you had in mind, or it may just turn out to be totally different.

So, all ideas are important to consider, because like the actor Christopher Reeve said in his book *Nothing Is Impossible*, nothing truly is impossible, especially when you put your mind to it either by focusing on the issues and the challenges or by having answers be the result of not even thinking about them. It truly is interesting how our mind works!

One point will be clear about your end product. You will have accomplished your goal to take care of your talent and your creativity, thus feeling fully satisfied.

KEY IDEAS TO REMEMBER

- Your life can be inundated with responsibilities, such as your job.
- You and your family are important to one another.
- You and your friends are important to one another.
- Weekends can be either very full or sometimes relaxing.
- Talent is "a special natural ability."
- There needs to be a designated time to develop your own talent.
- Balancing job, family, and friends is important.
- Creativity is "the act of being inventive and productive."
- Boundaries, including designated personal time and space, are essential to develop your creativity.
- If not your home, somewhere else needs to be considered to pursue your project.
- Creativity can arise anytime and anywhere.
- Your emotions can inspire your creativity.
- Nothing is impossible when you put your mind to it.

2

YOUR ABILITY TO BE TALENTED

You might have been raised in a family where freedom of expression was encouraged. You were considered a human being who just so happened to be young, but you were definitely seen and heard. Your opinions were respected. You were allowed to explore a hobby or to pursue an interest, so long as time and money permitted. If money was an issue, you might have had to work for what you wanted, but with your determination, you could pursue your hobby or your goal.

You might have been able to gain an appreciation of the global community with plays, museums, arts and crafts fairs, county and state fairs, people of various backgrounds, surrounding cities, your state, your nation, and maybe even different parts of the world. With such global opportunities, as well as through your exchanges with other people, you might have gained a great perspective of many aspects of life.

The major consequence for you as an adult would more than likely be that you felt enough encouragement, enough praise, enough inspiration, and enough determination to realize that you could succeed in whatever you wished to pursue, although you might have sometimes needed to earn money for your projects with the help of your parents or by working. You thereby became a person with a very positive attitude, with that much more talent, with that much more creativity, and with a dose of reality in the realization that it might take a certain amount of time and money for your project.

Such a positive environment is commendable and always needed.

On the other hand, it is possible that although you might have been raised in such a very positive environment, you might have felt inhibited. For example, your parents developed their talents as excellent musicians. They might have earned respect from family and friends. They might have earned respect from the local community. They might have even earned a lot of acclaim nationally and internationally.

You would attend many events in which they were renowned, and you were only considered as a person related to them. People might have asked you if you were going to follow in their footsteps or if you were acquiring the same talents to be on stage one day. In turn, you might have meekly responded with "yes" or "maybe," knowing that you would be continuously compared and contrasted with your parents and/or siblings.

There might have been certain expectations or hopes that you were told or that you only had heard throughout your developing years. You might have even tried to develop these same natural abilities that your parents exhibited to the best of your ability in order to feel satisfied with yourself or, at least, to be accepted by others. Indeed, you might have easily felt that you were always trying to play "catch up," meaning they always were better, and you always were trying to be at the same level of expertise and thus creating a lot of stress for yourself to excel.

You might have felt deflated by not achieving the same standard of success as they did. The subsequent lack of success might have snowballed negatively, and you might have then felt like a failure in practically everything you wanted to do. You might have then felt the dissatisfaction from your parents, even though they tried to be as encouraging as possible and to accentuate any type of minor improvement you made. Consequently, you might have been dramatically and emotionally affected for the rest of your life.

If you had siblings who you felt were much more gifted, your inner need to succeed might have been diminished by their successes compared to your attempts that were not necessarily successful or not to the same standards of the rest of the family and perhaps of the community. It could definitely have led to depression, anger, guilt, and shame for not achieving the same heights of approval from others.

If your attempts were successful, there still could have been many comparisons and many contrasts, making you believe you had not succeeded well enough based on the standards of your parents and based on how your siblings reacted possibly with scorn or with nasty, patronizing comments.

Another good example would be in terms of academic performance. If one sibling consistently earns high grades with ease and if another sibling tries as hard as he can but not to the same level of competency and success as the other sibling, there can be some major dissatisfaction. The "weaker academic" sibling could be told, "Well, your brother did so well. Why can't you? Try harder!"

While the first brother has an easier time with the material, the other brother has a more difficult time. Unless the parents understand that everyone is different in terms of their ability to do well, this enormous amount of comparisons and contrasts can have an everlasting effect on one's self-worth and on one's ability to be successful in whatever one wishes to pursue.

This author is also a tutor. While most parents are sensitive to not comparing their children, two parents shared with me that the younger brother was smarter than the older. The older brother was in the same room at the time they made this comment. Even though one sibling may actually be smarter than another, it is exceptionally important not to label. This can lead to a lot of hostility, inferiority, and superiority, all of which should be avoided as much as possible. Even if this is the case, people can improve when they are given the time, the attention, and the encouragement.

If you were raised in such an atmosphere where you did not necessarily meet or exceed the expectations of your parents and/or your siblings, please remember that they have been gifted to have their own certain talent, their own certain amount of creativity, and their own ability to produce their own standard of happiness.

You are gifted in so many ways, and your proclivity is totally different. Their path is different from yours, and, if they gain an appreciation of your gift, fine. They may gain a newfound sense of respect for you for coming to this conclusion, that they may be unable to do what you are capable of doing. If they do not, fine as well. We are all unique in our own ways, even though there are certain things about all of us that we have in common.

You and only you can determine your own life path without anyone else's expectations. It is important for you to be happy with how you are and with what you wish to do as you grow up and when you are an adult. After all, it is your own life that you are painting as your masterpiece.

Of course, you may encounter a mentor for whom you have a lot of respect, because he or she sees you wanting to learn. He or she will not regard you as being lower than what you justifiably deserve. You really do deserve to develop and to blossom in your own endeavors in your own time.

This author encountered a high school student whose family background was definitely less than desirable, with him being influenced by a gang. His family moved him and his younger brother to another relative. At the older brother's high school, a teacher inspired him to get involved with film photography. Eventually, he and another student entered some film competitions for youths in their county, and the two of them won the top honors two different years. The older brother is now in the university, fulfilling his dreams of creativity in music, and the young brother is attending a local college with his career to be determined.

You might have been reared into believing that you would not become anything in your life. You might have been told that you were not educated enough. You might have been told that you probably would have some sort of menial job for your entire life.

All of these abusive comments could certainly have deflated you emotionally. You could have been brainwashed by these people. Indeed, you could have lowered yourself to these negative expectations, and you could have become more depressed. Then, they would see that they were right. Their prophecies would have been fulfilled.

Your personal life and your job would have become a reflection more about them and their attitudes about life and about you rather than how you truly are as a human becoming. In fact, these individuals would have drastically tainted your future, and they certainly were not being respectful, encouraging, or praising of your individuality.

You may have been abused emotionally, mentally, physically, and/or sexually, the very things that nobody should ever encounter or deal with. You could have become so distraught by someone else's actions that you might have decided to remain the victim of your circumstances. In turn, such a result could easily have remained imprinted on you for the rest of your life.

This author, having taught and tutored for over forty years, has worked with many students. One high school student considered herself "a holy terror" because she was acting out her frustration on all of her teachers, except not with me. I continuously showed her respect as a person along with being a student. It is due to my positive attitude and my respect for her that, to this very day, she still is in communication with me and considers me her father.

Being human, one tends to make sound judgments along with mistakes. The sound judgments become a validation and an energizer in order to help you succeed that much more so in your life, and you are to be congratulated for these positive outcomes.

On the other hand, mistakes do not define you. Of course, they can be a letdown for you and perhaps for others around you. What you have learned from your mistakes in order to become a better person is exceptionally more important. Of course, there probably will be consequences to your mistakes, but it is not the end of the world. It is the beginning of a new world, a realization of how much you have learned in order to become a better person through your life experiences.

In actuality, such mistakes can become your gifts. After the initial letdown that can naturally take place, you can understand the errors of your ways, and you can make the appropriate decisions as to what will possibly become successes instead. In turn, such consequences can become your guides to a better future.

Even if there might have been parents accentuating the negative instead of learning from one's mistakes, there might have been one encouraging remark by someone, like a teacher, an adult in the community, and/or a friend, who could have been such a spark of encouragement or a highlight in your life that you were able to disregard your family's negative perceptions. Thus, you might have been enlightened to excel.

It is hoped that your family's disapproval would then have shifted to a better respect for you and an understanding that you needed to mold your own future. If they were totally accepting and loving of you, they would have appreciated and accepted you for who you were instead of who they projected you to be. If not, it would be their problem. Under such horrible circumstances, you could easily diminish your respect for them, although you would love them, because they are your family.

It is always important to realize that you are a separate individual from any negative individuals that have been or may be in your life. You may not be able to change their minds, but that is not essential. You are essential to your own self. You have the power to change your way of being, thinking, feeling, and evolving your own present circumstances as well as your future. You are your own person, and that is all that truly matters.

Throughout your educational years, you had been taught the basic information of reading, writing, and math. There were times in which you were able to expand your knowledge by creatively thinking, asking questions, and coming up with conclusions by yourself, especially in such classes as English, history, art, science, debate, and/or speech. While this was good and helpful, now is the time to expand on your own creativity, perhaps with a class of your own liking, without any stigma or label of grades or the pressure to excel.

Something noteworthy for your consideration is the field of technology and your own creativity. Technology can give you a great deal of flexibility. A lot of creative designs can be made with a computer or a laptop, with software programs and apps, and based on your own talents and abilities. It is important not only to use the most suitable programs involved, but also to explore the other programs already in a computer or a laptop so that you understand its full potential and can develop that much more flexibility and creativity for yourself.

If internal programs of your technological device, software programs, and apps are not available, it is appropriate to explore your options: to upgrade your computer or your laptop by adding more memory, to download programs for free and/or to purchase the most appropriate software programs and apps that can assist you, as well as to attend classes to find out what other possibilities are available for you to consider and to use.

If and when you are in the market for a new technological device, please be sure to check all kinds of smartphones, laptops, desktop computers, and tablets. On the internet, you will be able to find a way to compare and contrast these technological devices for their costs and for their uses. Smartphones have evolved tremendously and are very handy when you simply wish to post ideas later on to use on other technological devices.

Laptops and tablets are also quite handy due to the fact that you can transport them.

Desktop models are quite handy, if you prefer to have one space all the time where you can devote yourself to your work. The advantages of desktops are that you have a much larger screen on which you can have multiple windows for various uses, and desktops typically have more memory. There may be other advantages based on the brands themselves.

Of course, if you have the money for it and if you have the need for it, you just may wish to buy many of these technological devices with Wi-Fi. In this way, wherever you are, you can do your work, such as in your office or anywhere else. Then, you can email material to your desktop so that you can continue working at your home on your desktop, if you wish.

After deciding which technological devices you might prefer based on your needs and wants, please decide which stores have the technological devices you wish to compare and to contrast. In this way, maybe you need to go to one or two stores only, because that takes a lot of time and gas. Also, you can save some money, which is always nice to do!

At the stores you go to, it is very important that you devote time by yourself with the possible technological devices so that you will not feel pressured by anybody to buy any particular model. After all, this is a personal decision that only you can make. In this way, you are able to determine which technological devices will suit your needs to the fullest. If it means devoting an hour at the store, so be it. It is your money. If a salesperson approaches you to find out if you have questions and/or concerns, it is advisable to say "not now" so that you may resume your own search of the technological devices you are contemplating to purchase.

If and when you do need the assistance of a salesperson, you may wish to say that you do know the major functions and also to mention what your ultimate goals will be for it. You may also wish to know its limitations and what additional accessories may be needed to fulfill your needs and wants and their costs.

If you wish to purchase a printer, please be sure to check on the internet and in stores. One thing that needs to be remembered is the compatibility to the technological devices that you wish to purchase. Most of the time, this will not be an issue, although it is always best to ask for the best possible printer along with finding out about its functions.

Another thing very worthy of consideration is the options available on the printer, such as the ability to copy and at what speed, the quality of printing, the cost of the color and the black and white cartridges, fax and scan capabilities, wireless function, the ability to print on both sides, and any other feature that you may wish to have, such as 3D printing.

It is important to note all the advantages and all the disadvantages of each printer you consider so that you will be able to make the best judgment for your known needs along with any other features that would be worthy of your consideration.

Again, once you are at a store or at different stores, please be sure to focus your attention on details of each printer in order to make sure you get the best product at the best price for yourself.

Something else to consider is your family's devices, including everybody's smartphones, desktops, and tablets. It would be a good idea to write down the kinds of technological devices and model numbers your family already has, so that you can inquire about their compatibility with the devices you wish to consider purchasing.

While technological devices, printers, software programs, and apps are very valuable, they are only tools. The technological devices have been designed to fulfill purposes, to be your servants, if you will. They will work with you based on what you wish and when you wish to accomplish your projects. Your software programs and apps can be essential tools to elevate your ability to create whatever you wish. Nevertheless, your mind is the best creator, and your mind requires time and effort to develop your ideas fully.

It should be remembered that there is no time limit to create your talent, if it is a project that you are entertaining on your own without any responsibilities from your profession. You don't need pressure to create. Nobody is demanding that you complete your work within a given timeline. As a matter of fact, the more pressure you put yourself through in order to create, the lower your chances of creating to the fullest of your potential. Creating needs time, nurturance, and patience.

Of course, if you are required to create for your profession with time constraints, that truly does place stress upon you since the product is needed for the sake of the company, for the sake of the job, for your living expenses for yourself, and possibly for any significant others. Of course, if you are given a reasonable timeframe for your computer work, fine, although it may not always be the case, or it may take longer to complete your work than predicted.

If you are able to achieve while under this kind of pressure, you have an amazing skill that can help you. There are people who thrive under pressure and thus do better under pressure, and that is great. If not, please do the best you can under the circumstances, and, once you have completed your project that you feel will fulfill the expectations for your work, present your project for review.

Set yourself in the right frame of mind or mood for your creative project. It is interesting that when you develop your mind in terms of music that is being played, you are able to imagine things more creatively. If soft music allows your mind to work creatively, so be it. If loud music allows your mind to work creatively, so be it. In other words, if you like listening to music, consider the kind of music that will allow you to think more freely so that you can focus in the most efficient way. On the other hand, if any kind of music will be more of a distraction than a help, please consider no music at all.

One possible way to exponentially increase your mind is to learn how to play the piano or to perfect your piano playing. Of course, you need to learn how to read notes. You need to be a multitasker by reading the notes for the left hand and the notes for the right hand. It takes a lot of eye and hand coordination, which can translate into more usage of your brain to see the full scope of the final piece of music.

If you can learn by yourself, fine. If you prefer to learn with the help of an instructor, it is best to check with friends and/or family members who have had piano instructors, the local university's music department, or the local orchestras or symphonies for possible instructors and references.

Of course, if you prefer to learn how to play another musical instrument, so be it. The idea is that you will be able to learn how to produce music, which is a very good accomplishment; it can be very entertaining for yourself as well as others around you, and quite possibly have an indirect way of helping the creative side of you.

One method of having your own space and your own time—as well as to possibly become that much more inspired to create—is to undergo acupuncture. While the idea of pins piercing your skin may not sound too appealing, it truly permits you to relax for a while and energizes you that much more. As for the pins themselves, they feel like you have been gently poked.

Your acupuncturist may suggest for you to attend acupuncture sessions on a regular basis for an extended period of time. When you purge any accumulated stress by relaxing for the amount of time determined by the acupuncturist, you are allowing yourself the opportunity to broaden your horizons and to think about new ideas or to perfect your established ideas.

Something else to consider to maintain and to flourish in your creativity is letting someone else at home help you fulfill your regular household chores, if you live with someone else. You may feel that only you can do certain tasks, including cooking or cleaning. Yet, you can supervise at first how he or she is doing until you are totally satisfied. Then, you can pursue your own interests carefree while allowing the other person to help you with the things you normally do. Perhaps this can be mutually beneficial, in that you can then provide time and space for yourself while the helper will gain a new skill or a new appreciation of what you have been doing.

It is important to sleep as well as you can at night so that you can feel refreshed during the day. This may be easier said than done, seeing that there can be many events taking place during any given day. In turn, it may be a challenge to fall asleep, let alone to remain asleep throughout the night.

In order to get to sleep more readily, it is best to allow yourself to have a good hour of relaxation prior to getting ready for bed. This can be a way to relax and purge your mind of the day's events to make it easier to get to sleep earlier.

If you do have the time and the inclination during the day to take a short nap, it should be encouraged so that you may be able to revitalize your body and your mind during the rest of your day. It is always best to have as much of a refreshed mind as possible so that your creativity will expand as much as possible.

If you do work, taking a short nap cannot easily be done; however, it is not impossible. During your breaks, you may be able to shut your eyes for a little while and become that much more relaxed. Of course, if you tend to fall asleep rather quickly, it is best to turn on your alarm clock on your smartphone as a reminder to wake up and to become alert enough to continue with the rest of the day's work.

If this is not possible, please consider just staring out into space, thus having a "five-minute vacation," a mental vacation that permits you to travel to any location or to think of anyone or anything that is positive in your life you wish for five minutes. What is nice about this mental activity is that it is totally free of charge!

Also, by setting your mind at ease with happy thoughts, you are allowing yourself to become that much more energized for whatever needs to be undertaken next. It may even spark that much more creativity and that much more enthusiasm for yourself.

Another possible way to rid yourself of any unnecessary stress in your life, thereby allowing your talent to flourish, is neuromuscular integrative action (NIA), in which you dance by yourself to emotionally soft music in a dimly lit room under the supervision at first of an instructor. You then dance around other people, but with no touching whatsoever. At the end, you eventually dance with a partner. NIA can also be very energetic with physically challenging activities. (For more information, visit https://nianow.com.)

NIA is a very unique way to be in touch with your emotions, to focus on your positive, happy ones, and to help release your negative, sad ones. There are variances of the NIA experience, and each instructor or guide may have a different approach; however, the end result will be to feel that much better. So, if you are interested in NIA, check the availability and offerings in your area.

Another possible activity for yourself is Pilates, which is a very empowering and a very strengthening activity. You develop ways to control your body with rubber balls, Styrofoam cylinders, and other equipment. You are able to train and control yourself in order to keep yourself balanced and to strengthen your body overall.

It is best to have the assistance of a private instructor at first. Once you have mastered the techniques well enough by yourself, which may or may not take a long time, consider taking a class with others. Overall, when you strengthen your body, you feel that much more in control of your own body, thus helping you improve your physical well-being and physical strength. By accomplishing this goal, you feel more centered about what you can complete and master.

By feeling that much more confident about your ability to control your physical movements, you are allowing yourself the possibility of feeling more positive and more rejuvenated, and potentially permitting yourself to become more creative in your project.

Another suggestion to consider is both physically and emotionally helpful, although it can be rather exhausting as well. It is called myofascial release therapy (MFR; see https://www.myofascialrelease.com, a combination of mild massage therapy and traditional talk therapy). There can be one or two professionals who allow you to either lie down on a table or to sit on the table in order for you to talk about anything you wish, whether it is personal or professional. It is a safe, confidential environment where you are accepted for who you are.

When involving yourself in this process, you may become deeply in touch with your feelings, thereby releasing or cleansing them so that there are no distractions for your creativity and for your project. In fact, by just expressing yourself, you may be able to resolve any issues, or, if you are so inclined, you may want to ask for suggestions. It does require a person to be totally open with his or her feelings, and that may be rather challenging, at least at first. Yet, it can be done when you are so inclined, especially after establishing a rapport with the professionals based on trust.

When your mind is free of more stress, there is a better likelihood of a release like a cleansing of your heart and your soul, thereby permitting you to attain more readily a sparkle, an enlightenment, and an idea.

There are many books that also provide a lot of thought and inspiration. The first one for your consideration is *How to Think Like Leonardo da Vinci* by Michael J. Gelb. Leonardo da Vinci was the master of inventions, and you truly can gain a lot of insight into his manner of thinking. This book contains many ways to help the creator, namely you!

The second book, *The Artist's Way* by Julia Cameron, is another great tool to learn by yourself or can be used in a class with various explanations and various exercises for you to ponder. It is definitely worth your time and your effort to delve into this book in order to thoroughly immerse yourself in your creative energy.

In the event you wish to work with a mentor, a guide, or an expert related to your creative project, if you know someone who can be a benefit for you, please ask him or her. You may even want to allow that person to collaborate with you. Otherwise, you may wish to seek assistance through a tutoring firm, such as WyzAnt (https://www.wyzant.com), which can be a great resource for you. Otherwise, you may wish to attend an adult school, a vocational school, or a college.

You may want to check your local phone directory and/or chamber of commerce for possible tutors. Another possibility is to do a Google search for people who can assist you; however, please remember that they probably will wish to be compensated for their time and their effort. Even if it requires some money to be expended by you, your creative project is worth the time and the money you invest in working with someone. The result may be very beneficial and possibly even very lucrative for you and for the other people involved.

If you do consider working with someone who is a community member or a family member, it is best to determine several things. How well do the two of you get along with one another? If there is a possibility of a conflict of any kind, it is best to select someone else. Also, even if the two of you do get along very well, how much time do both of you wish to commit to this project? If one of you does not have enough time, it is best to reconsider your options or to possibly delay pursuing this project until you both are able to do so.

You may want to ask for the assistance of a family member. In fact, it could even become a family project, if you are willing to allow others to work with you. Again, it is exceedingly important that you are compatible with this person, that you both are willing to make the commitment to do this family project, and that you both devote the needed time for such a family project.

If you wish to consider making your final product ultimately for the public use, it is well worth your while to consult with someone familiar with such endeavors or to do a Google search in terms of invention firms so that you can be given the appropriate guidance for this process. If you are so inclined, one firm that is very reputable and very supportive throughout the entire process of assisting inventors is InventHelp (https://inventhelp.com). Both time and money will be needed to pursue a partnership with such a firm. Of course, if you have a very good understanding about the business world, this is not a problem for you.

In the event you wish to pursue your invention without the use of an invention firm, it is then very important to hire a patent attorney. It is to your advantage to check with a patent attorney whom you possibly know or have heard about, or to check with the local bar association. Otherwise, please visit the American Bar Association's website (http://www.americanbar.org/aba.html) for referrals in your area.

It needs to be understood that developing and submitting the patent application can take as much as three years. If your patent application is approved, great. You may then proceed to check all the possibilities for selling your product to a company or producing it in a factory. Of course, this takes money, and it will take time to finalize development for production.

If your patent application is not approved or needs clarifications or revisions, it will require more time and more thought for you and quite possibly for your patent attorney. That is why it is extremely important to research completely all of the intricacies of your product and the patent as well as to check through the great resources of the internet and local, state, national, and possibly even international companies for similar products.

If there are similar products, it would be to your advantage to make your product that much better and that much more unique for possible approval by the United States Patent and Trademark Office (https://www.uspto.gov). This will definitely require more time, more work, and possibly more money.

If you are an artist who has developed your paintings, sculptures, or other works to the level that you wish, it is best to go through the patent phase, even though it is a lengthy process; it protects you and your projects.

When you are enthusiastic about your project for possible public use but money is an issue, you may wish to consider Kickstarter (https://www.kickstarter.com), for which you can submit your idea online. Potential investors search the site for projects they want to fund. Nowadays, this is an exciting website for your consideration.

Should you be a writer of any form of literature who wishes to have your work published, it is very important to follow the customary rules that are given by the Chicago Manual of Style (http://www.chicagomanualofstyle.org).

In contrast to products that need to be patented through the United States Patent and Trademark Office, when you have developed any form of literature, it is sacred in the sense that it is yours and cannot be copied without your specific consent. If a person uses any part or parts of your piece of literature without giving you credit, you can sue that individual.

When writing for a publisher, there are some basic rules that need to be followed. First, please begin by opening up a new, blank document. Second, using the tools of your computer, there needs to be a one-inch margin on the top and the bottom and on the left and the right of each page. Third, the entire document needs to be size twelve and Times New Roman font style. Next, the entire document needs to be double-spaced. Next, you need to use the tab key consistently when beginning each paragraph.

Next, after each comma, colon, semicolon, period, question mark, and exclamation mark, please only use the space bar once instead of twice. You may have learned to press the space bar twice; however, for publishing purposes, it is once. Please do not italicize much since this can be rather irritating for literary agents and publishers. Please do not use the bold feature or the underline feature of your computer. Please do not use exclamation marks loosely since your words are more powerful; however, if you are writing fiction of any kind, these marks can be useful for the emotional conversations.

As you type your paragraphs, please take into account that each paragraph should be no more than seven lines each. The reason for this is that readers prefer shorter paragraphs instead of endless amounts of lines.

It is very important to devote as much time and as much effort as possible to complete your manuscript. It is suggested that you think about your writing project as much as you can. Perhaps, when you are away from your computer, you can have a piece of paper and pen or pencil available to jot down your ideas or record them on your smartphone, so that when you do think of something that you wish to include, you then will be able to note your ideas and to insert them when you have the opportunity to do so.

It is also suggested that the reviewing, editing, and revising be done three times, at least. With the aid of your computer, you should easily be able to make any adjustments you wish.

While you are typing your document, your computer probably has the ability to determine correct spelling and grammar usage. If it notes that you have an error, it will underline it. If there are too many spaces between words, it will identify that as well. In turn, it is important to determine the options available for you so that you can write your document correctly.

Even after having typed your document to the best of your ability and being aware of possible mistakes while writing, it is best to consider using your computer's spell and grammar check option for the entire document. There may be even more mistakes for you to be aware of and to correct. While this may seem like a lot of extra work for you, it is much better for you to correct your own errors rather than for a publisher's editor to identify many of them and then return your document for you to review and to correct it entirely.

It is then to your advantage to ask people to read and to write reviews of your document, and please do listen to what is being stated. If you agree, great. You may want to ask how it can become even better. Please be sure to discuss what could be done to improve the document. If it is reviewed favorably, it is to your advantage to have the reviewers write several sentences for the back cover.

Incidentally, publishers oftentimes will ask you if you can contact someone knowledgeable in your subject area who is well respected. It then is a good idea to contact them in order to see if they can read and review what you have written for a possible foreword of your manuscript.

If and when your literary work is reviewed and if and when there are significant questions and changes that need to be considered, you can truly feel a gush of emotions. You may feel like a disaster, seeing that you have expended so much time and so much effort into your literary work. Then, someone is able to offset your literary work by saying it needs to be revised. Of course, this is disappointing, but it is not the end of the world.

Under the circumstances, it is best to consider all of the comments seriously after the initial disappointment. Then, it is best to review your literary work detail by detail in order to see the relevance of each comment made and to make any necessary revisions to the best of your ability.

Ultimately, each comment that has been made is a way to improve your literary work. It may take a little time or a lot of time; nevertheless, the process moves you closer to acceptance by the potential publisher and acceptance by the potential readers.

Once your literary work is completely finished with any editing needed, this is the appropriate time to begin your search for the best way to have your written work published.

There are multiple avenues to reach this goal. First, you could buy a book called *The Writer's Market*, edited by Robert L. Brewer, which is an excellent resource containing websites for literary agents and publishers.

There are two versions that you can buy that are published each year. The first version contains helpful advice for writers, the listings of literary agents and publishers, and numerous listings of magazines and contests. At the end of the book, there is an alphabetical listing of the literary agents and the publishers.

The second version, while costing a little bit more, can be better for you. It contains helpful advice for writers, the listings of literary agents and publishers, and numerous listings of magazines and contests; however, in addition, it contains an alphabetical listing of each specific literary agent and publisher with the subject area listed as well. For an additional, nominal charge, you can access their most current data online. So, it is very worth it to pay a little bit more. This version can save you a lot of time doing your research.

Another way to get the above book is to check with your local library in order to see if they have it available for you. Under the circumstances, it will be necessary to jot down notes you wish to take and to do subsequent searches online, because you will need to return this book back to the library after a given time period.

Of course, you can always do a Google search for literary agents and publishers on your own, and you will definitely find a multitude of pages for your exploration with no charge whatsoever. Nevertheless, it will be a lengthier process compared to the deluxe version of the mentioned book.

While there are many reputable, worthy literary agents and publishers, there are those that are only interested in obtaining your money and not interested in helping you very much. For your consideration, it is best to check the Preditors and Editors website (http://pred-ed.com), which contains an alphabetical listing of many reputable as well as many unworthy literary agents and publishers, amongst other resources. Their findings are based on the experiences writers have had. Also, there is no charge whatsoever.

If you choose a literary agent or two and have checked their credentials on Preditors and Editors along with a general Google search, then they are probably very worthy of consideration. Be sure to see what specific subjects or categories they will accept. For instance, if you have written a self-help book, be sure that they will accept self-help manuscripts. If they do not include this kind of manuscript or if they specifically state not to propose self-help books, please continue looking for another literary agent. Otherwise, it will be a waste of your time.

Once you have chosen literary agents that accept your form of literature, it is a good idea to develop a query or a promotion-type email that will be acceptable to them. For example, they may wish you to include reasons why your book is important to be considered for publication; your qualifications, such as what makes you an authority on this subject; and your contact information. If you overlook anything that is required, there is a very good likelihood that they will disregard your query.

Keep a document in which you type an alphabetical listing of all the literary agents that you have decided to send your information to with the date sent and with the response. In this way, you will not repeatedly approach any particular literary agent. After all, you don't want to repeat your work and to annoy them as well. It is very important to be patient and to wait for a response, which may take three months to a year, although it is easier said than done to be patient. The last thing you want to do is to annoy any literary agent when you wish to be represented by them.

Some words of caution are important to remember. Again, please be sure they will accept your kind of literature. Second, if they wish to be the only ones to be communicated with, it is best to adhere to their wishes. Third, please adhere to their strict guidelines, because if you do not, they will not consider you. Next, please be sure that your query is complete, with no grammatical or spelling errors, and that you are concise so that what you state is enticing and logical. It is only in doing so that you have a better opportunity of being considered.

If you do receive a positive response from a literary agent, you are to be congratulated! It is highly important to thoroughly read the contract in full. In fact, it may be to your advantage to hire a business lawyer to analyze the contract so that you will know exactly all of the legal ramifications. Obviously, if you have a very analytical mind, there may be no need to hire a business lawyer at all.

Then, please be sure to sign the contract by the time it is required. Afterward, you need to do a concise job of completing the requirements that will be found on the website of the literary agent and anything that he or she requests that you need to do based on your signed contract.

The literary agent will make decisions based on what will be the most appealing to potential publishers and to the reading public. Thus, you are allowing him or her the opportunity to fulfill the job necessary for you.

After the literary agent asks you to email or mail your complete manuscript, it will take time for him or her to read and to evaluate it. Then, he or she may suggest different ideas. It will mean that much more time to make the appropriate revisions.

Please do not take it personally that modifications may be needed., While this is easier said than done, the agent is in the literary market to provide a service to you, to the publishers with whom he or she associates, and to the public at large.

You need to remember that a literary agent's commission will be taken from the sale of each piece of work, and the publisher's commission will need to be taken from the sale of each piece of work as well. The remaining profit will be distributed to you as per your contract. Thus, your literary agent will have very high expectations of your manuscript.

Once the literary agent has read and accepted your manuscript, after any possible modifications, he or she coordinates your manuscript with potential publishers, and their books are usually at major retail bookstores throughout the nation and oftentimes internationally.

Upon being approved by a publisher with the assistance of the literary agent, you then proceed to complete the expectations of that publisher. Those expectations are usually delineated in a contract that needs to be thoroughly read by you so that you understand it completely. Again, it may be a good idea to consult with a business lawyer in order for you to understand all the legalities and so that you have the best possible contract for yourself.

The advantage of having a literary agent is that if and when your book sells very well and if and when you decide to develop more manuscripts, there is a very good likelihood that you can work with him or her again. In fact, he or she may wish to develop a contract with you for more books that you have or have not been thinking about already.

While it is very promising and very validating to have your literary work appreciated and eventually published with the help of a literary agent, it needs to be understood that literary agents are extremely selective. In other words, every literary agent is exceptionally critical and analytical as to the potential of all possible manuscripts. Thus, you are more apt to receive negative responses to your queries than positive ones. It is not a reflection on you, if and when you receive negative responses. It just means that there is a likelihood of another more accepting literary agent eventually. It is best to look for and wait for other responses.

If you receive negative responses from all literary agents that you have selected and contacted, there is a second approach for your consideration in order to publish your manuscript. You may wish to pursue a publisher directly.

Also in *The Writer's Market* are listings of publishers with their specific subjects. Most publishers will typically post their specialties and requirements for potential authors on their websites. Again, the more precise you are while fully and satisfactorily meeting their expectations, the better are the chances of your being published with them.

If you wish to put all your eggs in one basket, to be fully confident in one particular publisher, that is fine; however, approaching more than one publisher will give you a better likelihood of being considered by one of them. Also, if you rely heavily on one publisher and do receive a rejection, then you will need to pursue another publisher, thus requiring that much more time.

When having done enough research work for publishers and once you have been selected, you will earn more of a profit than if you work with a literary agent. Also, when and if you choose to publish once again and if it is in the same genre, you will have an easier time fulfilling their expectations, and the publisher will be that much more receptive to reading and subsequently accepting your manuscript.

The third possibility is to self-publish. It means that you will need to perfect your own book as fully as possible. It means photocopying and binding your book at your own expense. It means promoting your book at your own expense. Of course, with social media being so prevalent, it is easier to do so; however, it is a good idea to have your own website and your own business cards, and to work with newspapers, magazines, and even doing your best to be interviewed on radio and/or television in order to publicize your book that much more so, whether you self-publish or not.

The fourth possibility is to seek a vanity publisher. That usually means that you share the costs of publishing your manuscript with the publisher upon being selected. The prices will vary based on the publisher.

There is another possibility to consider, and that is the e-book publishing world. With the technological advances that have been made with e-book devices to download e-books, this form of accessing reading material has gained a lot of popularity and is actually in more demand than printed books due to e-books being the most cost effective. That is why many publishers of all kinds offer hardbound books, paperback books, and e-books to their readership.

E-book publishers can be easily accessed by way of the internet. The major difference and major advantage with e-books is the fact that your e-book can be made available much quicker than by a regular publisher.

One of the major disadvantages with e-books is that they are not in printed form. There are many people who prefer to hold their books in their hands, to mark the pages where they stop, and to highlight sections by hand. Another disadvantage with e-books is that there are many readers whose eyes become strained from constantly reading on their smartphones, tablets, laptops, and desktops.

There are many other drawbacks to e-books from the author's perspective too. Since there are so many more e-books than printed books, you are in competition with a multitude of e-book authors. In order to be competitive with other e-book authors having written in the same genre, you probably will need to price your e-book comparable to their e-books.

Another disadvantage is the advertising element. Traditional publishers have a multitude of ways to advertise and to entice sales, such as different organizations and conferences. For e-book authors, it means a lot of time to reach different organizations and conferences and many times having to advertise by themselves, instead.

If you wish to have a wide market base for your book, it is best to work with a literary agent. If you want to have a somewhat large base of marketing your book, your best option may be to go directly to a publisher, and that will mean more of a profit for you. If you intend to just please a certain small market of readers, self-publishing can be your best option. If sharing the cost with a publisher is fine with you, a vanity publisher will suit your needs. If e-books are acceptable for you, that is fine.

No matter which method you choose to pursue, please be sure to involve yourself very thoroughly in the writing of your project. It may take six months, a year, two years, or even longer. The idea is that your masterpiece needs to be perfect and is a reflection of your sincere desire to express whatever you wish so that others will be able to fully enjoy what you have to offer. There is a definite advantage to this, because if you choose to develop a sequel or another book, if your first book is successful, you are apt to have a following that might even grow larger, which is always nice, to be sure.

It is important to have book signings at various times, and it needs to be your judgment call as to the time, the day, and the location. It is suggested that you limit the amount of book signings that you have during a given month so that you can take it easy. After all, you want to feel refreshed and positive for them. Also, if you intend to write more manuscripts, you definitely need the time to focus on your ideas.

You may want to give a workshop or a reading of part of your book in order to promote your book. You may even want to consider attending conventions and bookfests in order to give presentations there.

KEY IDEAS TO REMEMBER

- Your family is influential as to how appreciative you are of the world around you.
- Comparing and contrasting siblings will not help their self-confidence.
- You are uniquely gifted.
- Mentors can be highly influential.
- Mistakes can be disguised as gifts to help you learn that much more.
- Technology is a great tool, although you yourself still need to develop your mind.
- There is no time limit to create your talent.
- Playing a musical instrument can help your creativity.

- Being kind to yourself with acupuncture, taking naps, exercising, reading books, and having tutors and mentors can help your creativity.
- Developing a product can possibly be lucrative.

3

THE RAMIFICATIONS AND THE PURPOSE OF YOUR TALENT

The importance of talent is all around you. The conveniences of humankind are the result of people thinking "outside the box" or creatively as well as pondering the possibilities of design for our lives. Let's take a look at some examples.

Leonardo da Vinci was definitely a superb human being that had the ability and the foresight to develop many things that were far ahead of his time. Above and beyond being an artist with his *Mona Lisa*, he was interested in flying machines, solar power, anatomy, and civil engineering, just to name a few notable things. He produced much for our world in the fifteenth and sixteenth centuries.

Thomas Edison is very worthy of consideration. Due to his creative mind, he used his talent to invent the phonograph, the motion picture camera, and the electric light bulb in the nineteenth century. It was due to his ability to believe in himself that he developed these ingenious items that we have taken so much for granted for such a long time. While his original ideas may be considered primitive by our modern standards, he truly brought much to modern society due to his dedication.

Dr. Giulana Tesoro was a famous female inventor of the twentieth century who had more than 125 patents in the field of fiber and textile chemistry.

Orville and Wilbur Wright designed and successfully launched the world's first airplane. They saw the potential of aviation with the pure thought and creation of a device to take people into the air for traveling, just like how birds fly in the air.

Over the years, bigger and better forms of flying machines have been developed with the surge of airplanes, jets, helicopters, drones, and space exploration. It was due to the Wright brothers and many other people since who have helped our lives by transporting not only us from one location to another, but also goods of all kinds.

When we drive our cars, it is due to the creative minds of people such as Henry Ford, who developed the assembly line technology of mass production so that we can transport ourselves by means of cars and trucks instead of relying upon the horse and buggy of yesteryear.

Mary Anderson is very noteworthy for consideration, because she invented windshield wipers for our cars that are very essential for rainy and snowy conditions.

To facilitate the flow of traffic, we are guided by traffic lights as well as cameras monitoring whether we are in compliance with traffic laws.

Also, many cars have GPS to guide us to areas unknown to us.

In this modern day and age, we take so many other things for granted, like all of our technological devices, including our smartphones. In fact, these devices are so ingrained into our culture that we cannot seem to live without them.

Nevertheless, there are some distinct disadvantages to our modernization. There are many people who become addicted to one form of technology or another, or at the least enthralled with it. With advances in the field of smartphones, texting has become an easy, quick method to communicate; many people feel it is better than actual face-to-face conversations. In fact, there are many people that feel that texting is less confrontational and prefer texting.

The disadvantage of texting instead of face-to-face conversations is that we can read and thus interpret words differently. Thus, when we emphasize words that are not intended to be emphasized, misunderstandings can be the result. When and if there are questions from either person, there is no instant way to communicate with them without sending another text. If the respondent is then unavailable, delays will cause time to pass and for possible emotions to surface that were not intended.

There are many individuals who text and drive; innocent people have been injured, and there have even been deaths, unfortunately. That is why there are laws against texting and driving.

Even with the use of Bluetooth, in which people use earplugs to conduct conversations, this is still a distraction from the act of driving.

It always needs to be remembered that a car is a big machine that can be easily maneuvered. One slight change of the wheel can have a dramatic result in terms of where the car will go.

Even if a person does not use a smartphone for talking and texting, if there are other people in the car, engaging in conversations can have unusual side effects. This author knew of a competitive teacher who had a very bad temper. One year, his team of high school students did not do well at a competition. The students were dismayed by the results whereas the teacher was furious. They drove away in their van, and the teacher began to use very foul language due to being so very angry. The students were all very quiet, realizing that they could have done better.

He continued using foul language as he was driving the van, and he evidently did not realize where he was going. When he calmed down for a moment, one of the students mentioned tactfully that he was going in the wrong direction in order to go to their home school. With disgust, the teacher did not say anything to that student. He made a U-turn and proceeded to take them to their home school without ever acknowledging what he had done.

The obvious reason for sharing the above story is that distracted driving of any form can create situations that can create not only embarrassment, but also situations in which there can be unforeseen dangers, such as a person on a bicycle or a pedestrian having the right of way and becoming injured or dying from a distracted driver.

Another unforeseen, possible danger of smartphones is less pronounced. We can initially post phone numbers of individuals and companies along with their names in these devices. When we wish to call them, we can become so reliant on our address books that we actually do not know the phone numbers, or we can press a key and say the names of the individuals and companies so that they are called automatically.

You can easily lose your ability to memorize phone numbers, unless there are specific people whose phone numbers you have known for years. The people who are close to you, such as family members and close friends, will be easy for you to recall. The people for whom you work, if you work for a company, for example, will be easy for you to recall as well.

Consider memorizing *all* of your phone numbers so that your brain is constantly being active. You may think this is an impossible task to complete; however, nobody is giving you a definite time to complete this. You may wish to memorize only a few each day. After a week, you may wish to review what you have memorized already. Eventually, you will have memorized all of your phone numbers.

Along with memorizing phone numbers, it is also suggested that when you need to do some errands, you create a list prior to leaving your home. Put this list in your pocket or in your purse where you cannot necessarily look at it. Then, consider completing your errands as well as you can without this list. After completing as much as you can remember, it is a good idea to check your list in order to see what you remembered and if you have forgotten anything.

There is definite reason why doing something like these suggestions is important. By doing such memorizations, you are using your brain. In turn, you are going to be able to memorize things that much more readily.

A nice side effect can be that you can become that much more creative. When you are continuously using your mind to think, you are lessening the chances of getting dementia and Alzheimer's disease. It is not a guarantee, but it is always worth the chance. Another positive effect of memorization is that it can inspire you to want to learn more things about life.

There is a 1970 science fiction movie entitled *Colossus, The Forbin Project* that deals with how a man devised a computer system that could basically control society's functions so that humankind could focus on loftier goals. Despite this good intention, the computer Colossus eventually controls everybody.

While this is obviously pure science fiction fantasy, the overall message is that we must learn to use technology as a resource and not as something that we become heavily reliant upon. Also, we may become so dependent on all of our technology that we will feel lost without such technological advances.

The moral of this movie, as well as for our lives, is that moderation is the key element to always consider practicing. Technology has its purpose and function that can enhance our lives, but we must continuously seek a balance and use it in ways that still allow us to be self-sufficient and able to relate to one another in compassionate, sensitive, and sensible ways.

A more recent movie entitled *Her* (2013) deals with a shy, lonely man who wants to connect with a woman, any woman, but feels inhibited. He eventually turns to a computer program with the voice of a woman. He feels very connected to her, so much so that he becomes reliant on her. It is only after a while that he realizes that she, this computer voice, has done the same thing with many other men throughout the world. Finally, he connects with a live woman.

In the medical field, there are operations that are now being performed with the assistance of robots.

In the automotive field, there are self-driving cars in order to make sure that driving is more accurate, although this is a field that will need more refining for it to be possible and for it to be accepted.

There have been experiments in which families have tried to live without technology for a two-week period of time. You can only imagine how there can be major misgivings to volunteer in such an experiment. While there has been resistance, particularly from today's youth, they eventually learn to enjoy the freedom of being without technology. Families begin to communicate with one another in a better fashion and have a better appreciation of one another.

At the conclusion of such experiments, a lot of families return to their technological devices. Depending upon the individuals, they either return to this addiction completely; only use the devices moderately, but not to the maximum extent as they had done previously; or they do not wish to indulge in such devices, unless they are students whose teachers require them to have internet access for their communications and for their studies.

When families go on camping vacations where there is limited or no internet access, this can be a very trying time for family members who wish to connect with their friends and other family members. Also, if the parents are interested in knowing what is happening with their work, having some sort of communication is going to be like an addiction.

On such vacations or any other area where there is limited or no internet access, it always needs to be remembered why you are on vacation, which is to have deserved time off from your regular responsibilities and to enjoy the people and the surroundings. This is easier said than done. Youngsters may feel bored by not being able to text and to be linked to their social media, although it will eventually seem like a vacation from the world of technology.

Advancements for all of humankind definitely deserve to take place on a regular basis. You have imagination to assist in this process. You need to remember that people's lives can improve. At the same time, it would be ideal to make sure that these modern conveniences enhance not only life, but also people's ability to communicate with one another more easily, if possible. People's lives will thrive and be that much more joyous individually, interpersonally, and professionally.

Devices will come and go. The innovations of each one will last for a while. Then, more innovative devices will surface, making the former devices obsolete. Also, even if specific devices become the so-called norm and supposedly cannot be surpassed, human interaction and face-to-face communication are the essentials of happiness, not the very best technological devices.

Creative people are providing a service to others. Of course, these designers may be benefitted due to the fact that they may become famous and wealthier, able to support their own lifestyles. Some great examples of people who have made a major difference in people's lives are self-development gurus Rhonda Byrne, Wayne Dyer, Anthony Robbins, and Oprah Winfrey. A book worthy of consideration to read or to read again is *The Secret* by Rhonda Byrne.

Ultimately, these designers and forward-thinking people are the harbingers or the inventors of our modern society today and for our future. Their ideas once developed are the springboards of future ideas by more people in society.

Thus, please allow yourself the time and the space in order to become creative, because you can become a valuable influence to others. It may take a little time or a lot of time. In either case, remember to be patient with yourself. The major side benefit is an increased sense of satisfaction. You too may be able to make a tremendous, positive impact with others for that much more of a fulfilling life. Lastly, please sparingly use the internet so that you can develop your own creative styles of ideas that can be worthy of consideration by others, although it is always important to balance your personal pursuits with your personal relationships.

KEY IDEAS TO REMEMBER

- The importance of talent is around you.
- Modernization has its advantages and its disadvantages.
- Memorization of phone numbers can keep your mind active.
- Creative people provide a service to others.
- People are much more important than technology.

II

The *Emotional* Elements of Your Life

4

YOUR FAMILY HISTORY

If you reflect on your experiences from your childhood days, you may feel many kinds of emotions.

While it may be challenging to remember the first couple of years of your existence, those memories are ingrained in your subconscious mind. Eventually, through meditation, hypnotism, a fleeting thought leading to an early occurrence, or any combination of these methods, you may remember fragmented moments that really impressed you in one way or another.

It is funny how association can spark memories or thoughts of yesteryear. You may reflect on some baby photos of yourself, thus quickly getting a glimpse into a childhood memory that may or may not be related to the photos themselves. There may have been a favorite relative, like a grandparent who would give you extra treats when he or she would visit, who comes to mind just by your looking at a totally unrelated photo.

You may be doing something entirely different when a memory suddenly surfaces, a memory of something insignificant, something endearing, or even something extremely detrimental. You could be driving in your car. There is a song or a sign, for example, but nothing that can be associated with the sudden memory. There is no rhyme or reason for it to happen, but it does happen.

You may remember when your parents would carry you in a stroller in the neighborhood. You may remember and cherish those times when you felt loved, held, and sung to, validating the fact that you belonged and were loved in the family. You may remember those wonderful times when you could not wait to be fed by one of your parents so that you would get his or her individual attention.

While these kinds of positive memories are about the distant past, you probably do have many more vivid memories from later childhood, when you became much more alert to your surroundings, when you matured, and when you were able to reflect on your circumstances. You were older but still in the home environment of your parents.

All of these recollections or flashes of the past are very instrumental for you to ultimately become the person you are, and they may even lead you to other thoughts that can be very positive for you and for others around you.

On the other hand, while you may have many fond times of the past, there may be instances in which you remember the negative occurrences that have culminated in you becoming the person you are, possibly a fractured individual emotionally.

You may remember the time that your parents seemed to be shouting at one another, and, although you did not know why they had been arguing, all that mattered was that they seemed to be hurting each other emotionally, that they were threatening the stability of the home environment, and that you may have felt a tremendous amount of fear about what was taking place. In fact, you may have interpreted their arguing as meaning that you somehow were the cause, thus creating a guilt complex within you when their verbal battle with each other had nothing to do with you whatsoever. In other words, you could have easily internalized such negativity.

You may have heard or seen your parents fighting so much that they began hitting one another, creating chaos between the two of them. Such hostility could have created much fear, anxiety, and doubt within yourself, when the only thing you wanted either consciously or unconsciously was to have loving parents. Again, you may have internalized their negative situation as meaning that you somehow were at fault. Perhaps you thought that if you were not around, they might not have been fighting in the first place.

You may have been in your car seat in your parents' car going somewhere. Everything seemed to be okay until you heard and felt a big crash. You felt squashed, a sensation that made you very uncomfortable.

Also, there were splinters of glass that hurt you, thus making you cry. Unfortunately, you were in a car accident.

These traumatic events could definitely make you react in different ways. You might have partially blocked these memories due to the intensity of these events for many years; however, you may suddenly remember. This emotional alarm clock, if you will, may create a feeling within you that may change your life completely, because you will have suddenly recalled an episode that you subconsciously were able to avoid with temporary success.

In terms of your parents' arguing, you might have reacted by not wanting to involve yourself in any kind of disagreement, because this would cause more instability in the relationship. Unfortunately, the human condition being as it is, there will be instances in which differences of opinions will exist, but you could make every attempt to avoid such confrontations.

In terms of the car accident, there could have been other kinds of ramifications. You may not want to ride or to drive in a car now that you are older, but not really understand why this is the case. You may not want to be around glass due to the physical harm that it created.

In other words, even though you were much younger and not necessarily aware of your surroundings, you could have been unconsciously aware of the impact of such events. If any kind of childhood trauma surfaced later on in life, you could possibly react in any number of ways.

Seeing that traumatic events can happen anytime in one's life, even while you are young adults or when you are adults, there can be any number of traumatic events that can and unfortunately do occur that truly can make an impact on your life.

Of course, if you are a youngster, you are much more aware of your parents, other relatives, and friends. In terms of your parents who may be arguing, it is almost like being captive in an emotional jail in which it may seem that you have no alternative but to remain in these negative circumstances.

Nevertheless, you may have heard the expression, "You can fool some of the people all of the time, and all of the people some of the time, but not all of the people all of the time." Eventually, your parents will be caught saying something or doing something when nobody appears to be listening or watching; however, the truth of the matter is that someone will be around. It is only hoped that when such conflicts do take place, you can leave your home in order to find some semblance of peace for yourself. If you and your family are out and about, of course, it will be harder to leave, but it is so very important for you to be able to have peace and stability instead of disharmony in your life.

A crucial ingredient to peace and stability in your own personal life is to love yourself and thus to keep yourself protected. This truly can either be the biggest uplifter, or it can become a major struggle to attain. Charles Dickens wrote in *Hunted Down*, "A very little key will open a very heavy door." Indeed, he is right. One small, positive glimpse into yourself can enlighten you to feel better, to have a better perspective about yourself and about others.

While this may sound very flowery and very unrealistic, it can be done. You can have a positive attitude in order to help yourself become that much more realistic and creative in your personal and your professional endeavors. In turn, you can be more receptive with everyone you encounter.

One thing to always remember is that where there is life, there is hope. So, it is important to be patient with yourself. Change of any form does take time. Feeling better does take time, seeing that it probably has taken a considerable amount of time for you to feel the way you do right now. You may have tried to just live in denial until you could no longer tolerate the situation. Then, you would reach out to a counselor, and that is very needed and very courageous to do for your own sanity.

After all, you deserve to be loved, to be reared in a positive atmosphere, whereby you are treated with the respect that every human being has the right to have all the time, no matter what your age is. Indeed, it is important to love yourself and to protect yourself. It may or may not be difficult to accept and to practice this concept, although being comforted and loved by others can be a way to help validate your beautiful self.

Also, if you have siblings living with you in a hostile environment, they too probably are the victims of abuse, and they are entitled to live positively as well. Under such circumstances, if you are an older sibling, it needs to become your loving duty to shelter them in any way you can, meaning to guard them from any form of abuse and to comfort them when there is fear that is prevalent. If you are the younger or the youngest of the siblings in a family situation that is rather hostile, it is best to work together with the older siblings for the sake of all of you.

There is another factor for being assertive in loving and in protecting yourself. Your parents are hurting emotionally, and they need help. They evidently have issues that they are contending with, because they are acting out in abusive ways, which makes it difficult for them to raise children. They may or may not become better parents in the future; however, they need to face the consequences of their abusive actions against you and possibly your siblings. Then, they need to work on resolving their own particular problems, ideally with a counselor, so that they can work them out rationally, without imposing their negativity upon you or anyone else.

If your parents are undergoing a divorce, there will be a multitude of emotions that they will be experiencing, and you will be experiencing a loss of the family you wish to try to maintain. Please try to understand that it is not your fault. There are issues that you may or may not understand that are interfering in the relationship between the two of them. They can no longer be in each other's company, and they wish to be divorced. Again, it is not a reflection of you personally whatsoever!

If you do feel frustrated or scared, which are very valid emotions to be experiencing under these kinds of circumstances, it is important for you to talk with one of your parents if at all possible, to confide in a sibling, to seek a friend to talk with, or to seek a school counselor. In this way, you have a way to vent and to express and to resolve your emotions.

Even though your emotions should never be discounted, your education should never be discounted, either. If your home represents stability, comfort, and love despite some natural disagreements at different times of your life, you can feel safe, generally speaking. You will feel emotionally secure.

You will understand that people can get into arguments, although they will eventually resolve their issues, thus restabilizing the family environment. You will be able to concentrate to the best of your ability in such an environment. You thus can naturally feel self-confident due to the love and to the support that your parents have solidified.

If and when there is friction in the home, your education needs to be the focus. You then need to be in a room in your home that is far away from where your parents are so that you can do the best you can to concentrate. If they are so loud that you cannot concentrate, it is best to excuse yourself, saying that you need to go somewhere to concentrate.

Perhaps such a comment from you will make them realize how they are affecting you, even academically. Perhaps they will stop or at least discuss their differences in a quieter tone so that you cannot hear them.

If they permit you to leave your home so that you can focus and study somewhere, it is best that you and they consider some options as to where you will go and when you need to return.

The only reason for bringing up the idea of the home climate is that by being able to focus on your studies, you will then be able to fulfill all of your academic obligations. Perhaps, even one of the subject areas is going to be influential as to what kind of career you are going to pursue. Even if this is not the case, learning the material needs to be the highest priority for any future career.

If your parents know any or all of your subject areas and if there is a need to ask them questions, you may feel better about asking them tactfully, since they will not be ignited with any kind of rage that they may perceive or use your question as a moment to release their irrational anger with you.

You may not wish to seek their help due to wanting to resolve your questions by yourself and due to their arguing. You wish then to become your own teacher. Otherwise, you will probably ask other classmates or your teacher, refer to your book, go to a website that goes along with the book, go to an app, and/or do a Google search for assistance in understanding your subject matter.

If there is a trauma that concerns specific people, such as bullies at school, you could possibly gain enough emotional courage to confront those individuals. Nevertheless, this is easier said than done. You would need to develop your own plan, meaning the appropriate time to discuss the situation with them as well as what you would like to say in order to express your feelings and the impact of their actions.

If you are able to have enough courage to confront the individuals, it is essential for you to think of how they will react. If they are known to be confrontational, reactionary, and aggressive, it is then best for you to have another individual or two, who know your situation and your past, to accompany you. You need to do the best you can to protect yourself, but also to be able to convey your thoughts and your emotions to the other people involved.

It is also suggested to list their actions and your emotions on a piece of paper so that you will remain focused, or you could rehearse your ideas in your mind or out loud in order to make sure that you will convey everything that you want to say.

While you may be able to express your emotions clearly, it is important to realize that the individuals will react in the ways they wish to. That means they may rationalize what had happened. On the other hand, they may actually confess and sincerely apologize for their actions.

If they express a sincere apology and if you feel that there is genuine remorse, you will have accomplished your goal. You will have relieved yourself of some of the pain that you have built up inside. It does not necessarily mean that you will be totally free of your pain, but you will have done what is right for you and what is fair for you, and that is all that matters. It is only hoped that they will become much more sensitive as to what they say and do and how you will react from that point on.

If they are unable to apologize and if they only rationalize their horrible actions to satisfy their own warped egos, that is too bad for them; nevertheless, you will have regained your precious self by building up your own self and by defending yourself from their negativity now and in the future.

Another valuable tool that can be very helpful for you is to write a letter to whoever it is, whether the people are alive or not. It is suggested that you write it instead of typing it since it will take more effort, thus possibly releasing more of your emotions more freely. If this approach is chosen, there is no required length for the letter. There is no time limit on writing it. There is no need for correct spelling or grammar. There only needs to be your willingness to write as much as you wish and as often as you wish.

Upon completing this letter describing the situation and your feelings, there are several things for you to consider doing with it. You could put it in a place where only you could read and reread it as often as you wish, based on your emotions at different times. You might want to revise it or to continue writing sometime in the future, just so you could write more details.

You could build a fire in your fireplace, crumple up the letter, and throw the letter into the fire as a way to let the past experiences go up in smoke literally. You could also stomp on it as much and as long as you wish, along with shouting as much as you wish, in order to express your anger and your frustration about this individual. If you do this particular activity, please be sure to do it when there is nobody around you.

If and when you wish to confront them, it is best to have a support system, such as a family member or a friend by your side. It is then best to read your letter out loud directly to them face to face. You will be able to emphasize words with all kinds of emotions that only you can convey. You can repeat any parts of your letter in order to emphasize the ideas that much more so. This is your personal opportunity to rid yourself of some of the justified pain that you have stored. What is important is that you will have written your letter to resolve the situation in your heart and in your mind.

As varied as the possible traumatic events are that may have affected your life, there is not necessarily a single solution that fits all. No matter what kind of issue that may have emotionally hindered you, it is important to realize that you are much more powerful than the negativity that you encountered. You are much stronger, although it may take a long time to feel relieved.

If you were to allow the anger or pain to continue within you, those responsible could continue ruling or dominating your life such that you would not be able to blossom. Under the circumstances, it would be similar to allowing this negative experience to continue permeating your life and hindering you from living the life you deserve now and in the future. It is also very well possible that if you are in a committed relationship and perhaps even with children, you may damage your relationship with them, consequently affecting their lives as well.

Another consequence would possibly be for your physical health, because this negativity could easily make you wary, to the point of hindering you physiologically with blood pressure problems and a tendency to overeat or undereat, for instance.

On the other hand, if you are the abuser of any kind to another person, this is another matter. You may feel that you were justified in your negative actions. They too may understand how frustrated you had become, thus necessitating your desire to lash out at someone else that was available.

Nevertheless, there can definitely be major ramifications for this action, even if it felt justified. That one single spark of abuse could result in the other person becoming very afraid of you and angry with you, and they will naturally be on guard when dealing with you all the

YOUR FAMILY HISTORY

time. They will not be able to trust you. They could even learn to hate you. They could learn not to appreciate and respect you and be cautious as to what they say and do.

There is another way you need to look at any negativity that you impose upon your family members. Let's say your marriage is constantly negative. Can you imagine wanting to live in such an environment for the rest of your life? Would you want to? Would you not want to do your best to leave whenever possible?

The negative consequence of being argumentative around your children is that they will learn very well that maybe the best possible way to resolve issues is to get mad. Otherwise, what they see as being customary is exactly what they may try to avoid doing when they are grown-ups.

Voiding some if not all of the emotional issues of the past or of your current life will be essential for your emotional well-being and the well-being of others around you. You will benefit, and innocent people will feel safe and secure. There can be security, trust, and respect, resulting in a more positive environment, a community in which people can also develop or improve their talent.

KEY IDEAS TO REMEMBER

- Your childhood provides many positive and negative emotions.
- For one's negative past, counseling can be very helpful.
- Where there is life, there is hope.
- When parents know the subjects that their children are studying, that can be very helpful for their education.
- Voiding some if not all of the emotional issues of the past or present will be essential for your emotional well-being and the well-being of others around you.

5

YOUR EMOTIONAL TIDES CAN INFLUENCE YOUR LIFE PERSPECTIVE

Whether raised in a relatively stable environment or in a relatively unstable environment, everyone is going to have their emotional tides based on their history.

When you are in the happiest of moods, everything and everyone will seemingly look perfect. Even if there are some so-called imperfections, you may tend to disregard them, because you are willing to overlook these peculiarities and to focus more on positive qualities of the individuals and situations around you.

You are choosing a more positive frame of mind. There can consequently be a certain steadfastness within you that allows you to focus on your determined goals in terms of your profession, for example. Belligerent people may not necessarily influence you negatively. In fact, you may find that by remaining positive in your thoughts and in your actions, you may be able to influence them, even if it is only temporary.

When you are able to voice some possible discontent with anyone in a tactful and respectful way, you are giving them respect, as every human being deserves. More than likely, they will learn from what they have done incorrectly; however, if they do disagree with you and if they are able to share why they have acted the way they have, they may respond in a tactful and respectful way as well. It is the approach that you take that will make or break your relationship at that point.

The consequences of such a positive mood by you with your fellow workers, with your family, and with your friends can have a very lasting effect on your relationship with them. Such positive interactions can have lasting effects for all concerned.

If you are tactful and respectful with someone who may be in a negative frame of mind, there can be the tendency of this negative individual to become defensive, possibly to the point of being abusive in their response.

When this negative individual reacts defensively, he or she will probably defend the actions in an irrational way. Thus, an argument over details may be the result. If it becomes a hostile discussion, it is very important to deescalate the situation by saying that you both need a break by not being in each other's company for a while in order to reflect on all sides of the argument. Then, it is best to resume discussing the situation in a much calmer way later on, if at all possible. Finally, it is hoped that both of you can resolve the issues so that the relationship is better, with both sides understanding one another better.

If, however, one or both of you decide to continuously bring up the issues, and if both of you opt to be determined not to resolve the situation, it is always going to be a smoldering fire ready to become a big fire again, just by one word, one snide remark, or a strange look. Then, nothing can be resolved.

When you are in a negative mood for whatever reason, even the slightest irritation that you experience, either personally or professionally, will feel as though you wish to irritate the person or the situation even more. The anger or perhaps even the rage is something that cannot be controlled.

We as a society unfortunately have encountered many instances in which people, due to any number of circumstances, have lashed out at those that have provoked the relationship as well as at innocent bystanders. While it is understandable to be mad at individuals, some sort of constructive change needs to take place without inflicting any kind of harm on others.

Think of it in this way if you tend to be in a consistently bad mood. When children unfortunately become ill, they will feel miserable. While they know that their parents wish to help them in the best ways to recuperate and as quickly as possible, it can become a major challenge for the parents. If the parents are ultra-sensitive and if they become easily agitated, they will not be tactful and will not be totally helpful for their children. The parents will become very offensive and say and/or do things out of pure frustration.

Meantime, the sick children will not recuperate any faster, and they will have learned an important but horrible lesson from this experience. They will realize that they do not deserve to be sick. When they do become sick, they will become fearful of their parents, who look upon them as being the culprits, thus feeling guilty for feeling sick, which is only one of those natural, unfortunate consequences about human beings, no matter what age we are.

So, what can you do if you are in a negative mood and if you encounter a disagreeable situation that could incite you? It is important to realize what the circumstances are and to be aware of the fact that it is not necessarily a situation you have created. Upon doing so, you may be able to think more logically and perhaps even more creatively in order to understand the situation more completely and to begin resolving it as well.

If, in fact, you are the reason for the conflict between you and another person, while you may wish to be defensive about your actions or your words, such a steadfast position will only prolong the division between the two of you. While it is easier said than done, it is important to reflect and to decide to make amends with the other individual. Then, there can be more of a sense of harmony with the issue being resolved.

What needs to be addressed is the reason for being in a bad mood, thus causing pain for yourself as well as possibly for others around you in your home, with your friends, and at your workplace.

If there are past issues that are now interfering with your life, you have a choice. You can allow the past issues to rule your life so much that you will not have the opportunity to be happy and to thrive personally and professionally. Granted, there are past issues that can be so insurmountable that you are unable to survive well mentally. You may "go through the motions" of living each day, but you are not giving yourself the opportunity to at least ease your mind and your heart of the pain and of the heartache of the past.

Whether the situation is mild or severe, you do have options available. A family member can truly benefit you, if he or she is a good, patient listener and if he or she may be able to give solid advice in order to help you resolve the issue. If you feel a family member is too close for you to reveal your situation, it is possible that a friend whom you know well and who knows you well could be extremely helpful. Should you choose this option, please be sure that he or she is a friend not at your workplace, seeing that you will be constantly reminded of your disclosure by him or her, and that may impair your judgment and his or hers as well.

When overbearing issues become such a hindrance to your emotional health and when your emotions are the result of someone's insensitivity, being able to trust the other individual is going to be extremely challenging to practice. Indeed, it hurts very much, and it may take you an extremely long period of time to accept the other person, whether he or she apologizes or not. It all depends on the authenticity of the apology and whether those words lead to consistent, positive change and thus hopefully harmony.

Under such circumstances, depending upon the severity of the situation, it may be a good idea to get a mediator, like a counselor, to oversee meetings that the both of you can attend. If the other person opts not to even consider getting counseling but you are receptive to getting individual counseling, then that will be a start. After all, change has to come from within in order to have change from without. Nevertheless, this is not going to necessarily mean that the other person is going to be receptive to any changes you have made. It may take many meetings, because there may be issues that have surfaced recently that may be the result of your past.

By thus relieving some if not all of the past issues, you have the amazing opportunity of improving your mood. This is not to say that this transformation will remain steadfast. It does mean that you will attain more control of your life in every aspect due to the fact that you are allowing yourself the opportunity to improve your life with a positive perspective. If so, there is always the possibility that you may become that much more creative in your personal and professional life. No matter what, it is important to be patient with yourself so that you can heal at the rate that is appropriate for you.

KEY IDEAS TO REMEMBER

- Everyone has their emotional tides in which we feel different emotions every day.
- Choosing to be positive is beneficial to feeling better.
- Having a mediator help resolve problems between people may result in better relationships.
- By relieving some if not all of your past issues, you have the amazing opportunity to improve your mood and thus become more creative for whatever your heart desires.

III

The *Community* Elements of Your Life

6

YOUR ATTITUDE AND YOUR EDUCATION

So much of your life can depend upon your parents' behaviors and attitude during your childhood years, as was explained earlier.

Your parents might have led you down the path of life to understand, to appreciate, to love, and to assert yourself in respectful and considerate ways as well as to help others to help themselves. There may have been creative dialogues in which they actually listened and accepted your opinions. All of these positive activities are life-affirming events that could have led you to become more self-assured while still respecting the rights and the opinions of others, even if you might dislike or disagree with something or someone.

Of course, there could have been disagreements between you and your parents. There would have been times when you definitely would have preferred something that could not be granted and had to accept the fact that you could not always have all of your wishes realized.

The overall consequences of such interactions were that you could have become a better-adjusted individual with the ability to think creatively and critically and with the ability to accept the realities of life.

It is important to acknowledge that we as the human race are imperfect at times. We strive to do our best in order to accomplish our goals without making mistakes. Accidents oftentimes do occur, but they are actually gifts, lessons from which you can improve in the future.

Parents might have degraded you partially or totally due to their own negative attitude about life and their defeatist and/or belligerent perceptions based on their own past experiences. They could have been very pessimistic due to their own circumstances. They might have had the best of intentions and loved you, but they imposed their negative attitude onto you.

Your parents could have abused you in one form or another due to having so much pent-up anger that they could only lash out their negative emotions by imposing their hate upon you, the innocent person. Unfortunately, there are many parents who act in this manner, only to make their children the innocent captives who truly deserve better, who need fair, realistic standards with major toppings of love.

Your parents may have hoped that you could become your own appreciative learner, your own talented person. You were thus taught to become a creative, critical person who could rely on others at times in order to seek support and in order to become more informed, if and when you chose to do so.

You might or might not have felt some pressure to excel due to your parents having already succeeded due to the pressure they felt from their parents, thus placing that same type of demand onto you in order to succeed. They might have indicated that you should earn the same degrees as they did, so that they could be proud of you and your accomplishments.

While a negative parental atmosphere is totally unfair and undeserving for you, having parents who might place exceedingly high expectations on you is also totally unfair and not deserved.

The first approach is negative, with you as the recipient being burdened with their belief systems. The second approach, although focusing on the importance of education, requires you to only live up to their expectations, thus fulfilling their own dreams and not giving you the opportunity to fulfill your own special purpose and joy in life that may not necessarily be the same as your parents'.

Parents in both of these situations might not even know how influential they have been, but the end result is the same. There is no latitude for you to be your own individual person, because you have not been offered the opportunity or the encouragement to develop your own interests.

It is no small wonder that your attitude about education could be so very well engrained by how your parents showed you the world. A Spanish philosopher by the name of José Ortega y Gasset wrote, "*Yo soy yo y mi circunstancia,*" or "I am I and my circumstance." Indeed, the environment in which you are raised truly influences you.

Baltasar Gracián, also from Spain, wrote a book entitled *El Criticón* (*The Critic*) about a man whose views about society are very negative. He is marooned on an island. He meets a native who learns about how bad civilian life is from this critical person. Eventually, the critic and the native are rescued and brought to the city. While the native did observe the negative elements in the city as described by his marooned friend, he also recognized the fact that there were many positive elements in the city as well.

While your family upbringing could have played an instrumental part in your development, it is also your choice and definitely your responsibility as to how you will either agree or disagree with your parents' assessment about you, life, and education. Like in Gracián's book, the native could have remained negative by only looking at life in a negative fashion. Nevertheless, he chose to have an open mind about what he saw.

Two particular movies show how detrimental parents can be. *Shine* is the true story of an amazingly talented pianist in Australia whose parents were verbally abusive toward him. He did excel and became very famous; however, his horrible childhood permeated into his adult life.

The second movie, *Tommy*, relates how a set of parents becomes so overwhelmingly powerful, so totally self-absorbed, and so self-serving that they fail to see the beauty of their own son. As he grows up, his self-worth is deflated, but later he transcends his parents' failings to become a better person than they were.

Family influence, especially if it is negative, may have affected your education. You could have felt, for example, that you could never measure up to the intelligent people you knew in school. So you took your basic classes and did average work because your perceived expectations were low, and your parents' view about you was possibly even lower. You may have thought yourself to be a "loser," thus not having the capability of transcending your existence.

Your teachers may have tried to see a bright, shining star within you who could learn, but you truly could not visualize yourself as anything but being an average or even below-average student. They may have inspired you somewhat for a while. You may have succeeded a little bit, but failed more often than not, thus perpetuating your downward spiral.

If you became resigned to continue the trend of living down to their expectations, leading to a life of stagnancy and negativity, it is to your benefit to talk with others around you in order to listen to and understand different points of view. It is hoped that encountering such individuals can make a permanent, positive change in your perspective about life. After all, there are many more good people in the world than there are bad people.

Out of respect for your great self, you deserve to live up to your own potential, regardless of any negativity that may have surrounded you. If you do not know what your own potential might be, it is kind to yourself to explore your options by taking vocational interest tests. In this way, the test results can demonstrate to you what kinds of careers would be the most enjoyable and challenging for you. Another way to explore different professions is on the internet.

Upon taking vocational tests and/or exploring different professions online, it is then best to make arrangements with employers to do some job shadowing. After getting the appropriate permission to do so, it is best to observe as much as possible without interrupting too much. Then, when it is appropriate to do so, ask questions to clarify what you have observed. Also, upon the conclusion of the day of job shadowing, it is best to thank each person who took the time to allow you to be there and to answer your questions.

However you choose to determine the type of profession you desire, it is very important to determine what qualifications are needed to attain the jobs you are interested in. Then, it is best to obtain the education and the experience to attain the jobs.

If time and money do permit it, please consider the information of this book in more detail, because there can be enlightenment, happiness, personal self-worth, and lastly perhaps even more money earned.

No matter how positive or negative your parents may have been, it is a matter of your choice as to how you are going to venture forth into the world. You are the painter who can draw anything on the blank canvas. You are definitely the designer of what your life is going to be like. You have a lot of control over what can be done, which can be self-affirming and worthy for not only yourself, but also for others around you, including your family and your professional world.

YOUR ATTITUDE AND YOUR EDUCATION

Indeed, your attitude determines your altitude. In essence, it is a choice to have either a positive attitude or a negative attitude. If you feel that you can have a positive attitude, you are allowing yourself the opportunity to expand your mind and to be receptive to all sorts of avenues of learning. You are taking the initial step to improve yourself academically and to have an exponential way of appreciating the world around you.

You are not dumb. You may not know everything, but you do have the opportunity to learn more, especially when your heart and your mind are ready and willing to take that extra leap into the unknown world that can be realized by simply viewing an educational catalog at a nearby adult school, vocational school, or local college or university, or on an online course catalog.

Dorothy from *The Wizard of Oz* was yearning to return home, but she never knew how. She was finally inspired by someone to click her own heels and to think about the comforts of her own home, and it was as easy as that. She succeeded in returning home, and you can make it to whatever you desire by accepting possibilities that can lead to newer, better opportunities of personal and professional growth and happiness.

With this attained knowledge in whatever subject you pursue, you can become a shining example to others, and you will have that much more to share with your family. Who knows? You may very well inspire your own children (if you have them) or other young people by becoming so knowledgeable in your subject matter that they too are inspired to pursue a career in that field of study.

Even if they desire to involve themselves in another avenue in their life path, they still will have been influenced by your enthusiasm and by your appreciation of educational possibilities. In turn, they will exhibit enthusiasm and appreciation in their favored fields, and that most certainly can make their lives feel that much more fulfilled.

Even your friends will observe how invigorated you are by this attained information. As a result, your life will feel fuller, and you will be that much more aware of the world around you.

Depending upon your job status, you may even be able to increase your regular wages in the position that you are currently holding by taking classes or workshops. Another advantage of increasing your knowledge by means of education is that there can be a job of a higher authority that may include wage increases. You may even feel that much more confident about yourself because you were able to learn.

This is good, so long as you remember that you are still a human being and that everyone always deserves to be treated with respect. The reason to be aware of this is that people can be easily approachable when they have a layman's job. However, when they have succeeded in becoming a manager, a boss, or an administrator, they feel very powerful and act the part of an almost dictatorial individual, the exact opposite of how they were previously.

When having a position of authority, it is always best to be realistic and humble by remembering that the people you manage are the ones on whom you rely for a successful business. They have their jobs to perform for your sake and for the sake of the business. When there is mutual respect, there can be mutually beneficial results. When there is mutual disrespect, this can easily result in a negative atmosphere and reduced productivity.

It definitely is to your advantage to have an open mind in order to be receptive to new ideas and to new beliefs, especially if you are the administrator of a business. Let's look at the following two people.

If person A is well educated and well informed, he or she can make specific judgments and conclusions as to what has happened in terms of current events, for example. He or she may not necessarily be influenced by biased news in any form of media.

If person B is not well educated and not well informed, he or she can be much more easily swayed to fully accept news in the media without looking beyond the potential biases of the media. Person B will accept someone else's viewpoint and not to be able to "think outside the box" in order to come up with conclusions for himself or herself. Of course, this individual may learn from his or her experiences, thereby changing his or her opinions slightly or dramatically.

Here is another specific example. If person A is well trained and opts to take more classes related to his or her work, there is a better likelihood of advancement. If person B is in the same field but chooses not to take classes due to not having enough money or any other reason, there is a better likelihood of remaining at a lower salary rate. Person A will feel that much more fulfilled while person B will feel that life is a never-ending struggle. In fact, person B may feel jealous, thereby possibly creating some or a lot of tension between the two of them.

If you are undecided about pursuing more classes, it is important to consider any family member or any of your friends who are very knowledgeable. How are they fulfilling their dreams? What outward signs do you see that show their education has supplied them with a better perspective about life and maybe the ability to have a better material life? It does not mean that having more education will equal more money and more material goods all the time, but there is always that possibility.

On the other hand, which of your friends seems not to have developed themselves in terms of their education due to low self-image, money issues, and/or any other possible reason that you are aware of? How are they as friends? How are they fulfilling their dreams, or are they just barely keeping up with their bills and complaining all the time?

If you are satisfied with your life and if you have fulfilled all of your goals, fine. If you wish to advance in your profession, setting goals that are realistically possible can help you achieve what you desire. If you have some or a lot of envy for someone who has advanced, this is a wake-up call to yourself that you wish to advance.

Thus, some sort of sacrifice needs to be made in order to reach your future goals, although it means being patient with yourself, because change can take time due to financial constraints and obligations and/or simply realizing that there are only a certain number of hours in the day. In turn, you need to relax and "smell the roses," meaning make quality time for yourself and for others who are meaningful in your life.

KEY IDEAS TO REMEMBER

- Your parental upbringing can be highly influential when it comes to your attitude about yourself and about your education.
- Out of respect to your great self, you deserve to live up to your own potential.
- Parental expectations, be they low or high, can dramatically affect you.
- Your attitude determines your altitude.
- Everyone deserves the right to attain the highest amount of education they wish to pursue.

7

YOUR EDUCATIONAL LIFE

Learning is an activity that requires a lot of time, a lot of effort, and a lot of practice. No matter what one's age is, this is the case. This is a great way to expand your mind for your own mental development.

When it comes to school-age children, it may or may not be a challenge to have them become educated. With the influx of technological devices, including apps, games, and social media, it has become increasingly more challenging to have them become more focused, because they may view education as "boring," but one of those "necessary evils" of life. It is thus the purpose and the challenge of both parents and teachers to use and adapt such technological devices in order to use them as creative tools to promote education in the best ways possible.

Public schools have a wide variety of resources or they might require students to have such technological devices as smartphones and tablets. Government standards and districts give teachers guidelines so that students have the opportunity to learn.

While such devices and guidelines can be very helpful, students are the amazing variable based on their personal lives, their ever-changing moods, their peers, and how they interact with their teachers. In turn, these challenges can be perceived as either a negative or as a positive. It can be a negative for teachers who may use all kinds of resources available to motivate their students, but give up due to their constantly diminishing returns, if you will, because the students don't seem to understand the material due to a lack of desire to learn or their wanting to have fun instead of memorizing information that can be useful for them to know.

Teachers may perceive these challenges as a positive in that they will pursue a variety of ways to improve their style of relating to their students. Teachers will also seek advice from fellow teachers and attend workshops in order to inspire their students to see the value of their subject matter.

Luckily, there have been and are so many innovative, positive teachers who have been determined to make a difference with their students, such as Jaime Escalante, who believed in helping students achieve their potential, no matter what their background may have been. (His work with students in East Los Angeles was the inspiration for the movie *Stand and Deliver*.) It is by making this personal difference with students, one student at a time, that teachers will become an inspiration, role models, so that their students' lives will be better now and in the future. Technological devices will constantly change, although students will always want to be heard and respected.

To make school more relevant to the needs and to the potential careers of students, schools have been making major shifts in their subject matter. In this way, it becomes more enticing for students, and there is a better likelihood of more students being more focused on what the schools have to offer.

Academies oftentimes specialize in majors that can ultimately lead students to possible future careers (or, after learning about such careers, they may choose something totally different). At the least, students are given the opportunity to be aware of their potential interest. Along with such classes, they learn the basic skills that all society members need to know as well.

Charter schools are another great option for school-age students. Charter schools are funded through the local school districts and county offices of education. Quite often, the class sizes are lower than in public schools, and that can be appealing to both students and their parents, who wish to have better communication between all concerned; smaller class sizes can help lessen discipline problems.

Homeschooling most definitely has its advantages and disadvantages. The advantages are that learning becomes individualized instead of having to account for other students in different classes. Homeschool teachers, who are typically the parents or teachers who come from outside the home, will give the students that much more opportunity to delve thoroughly, but also rather quickly, based on the drive and the determination of the students themselves.

When the teacher and the student get along well, this is helpful in the learning process. They will more readily ask questions, knowing that teachers devote their time specifically with them and for them.

Just to give you several examples of the advantages, there was one student who had been homeschooled through the seventh grade. She eventually graduated from a public high school after the eleventh grade and attended the university level with two majors and one minor. Another example is a student who was also very studious in a homeschooling program. He successfully completed three years of Spanish in less than one year.

While these two students are just sparse samplings, there are many other success stories and will continue to be more of them, because it is truly amazing how individual attention and individual time can result in fantastic results. Of course, there will always be exceptions; however, a lot has to do with the drive and the determination of the homeschool teachers and the homeschool students themselves.

There are some disadvantages in regards to homeschooling. If there is a personality conflict between the homeschool teacher and the student, this definitely can interfere with the educational process. Under these circumstances, it is best to consider a couple of options. First, it might be a good idea to hire a teacher or teachers from a local charter school, for example, to come to your home or for the student to go to a specific learning center on a regular basis.

Another definite disadvantage can be that one parent needs to be the teacher while the other parent becomes the breadwinner. This can become a major stress issue for the working parent, unless the working parent's job pays very well in order to pay for the family's normal expenses. Of course, if there is money available from the school district or from the organization promoting homeschool instruction, this can help offset expenses that may come up.

Even if there are no personality conflicts and even if there are no money issues, one homeschool teacher with one or more homeschool students can become rather irritating at times. That is just the nature of the human animal. Under such circumstances, it is best to have a variety of activities the students can work on independently to relieve some of the pressure that they feel.

There are some high school students who are so bored or fed up with the high school process that they either drop out, which is not a very good option, or they prepare, take, and do their best to pass the general education exam in order to graduate much earlier. They prefer to get on with their lives in whatever way they wish to pursue, such as getting a job or enlisting in the military.

It is sometimes interesting to note that such students, after having matured, will return to pursue an advanced education at a college or in adult school with a specific purpose, or they will wish to take classes not for a career, but simply for the pleasure of it in order to expand their knowledge of specific subject areas.

No matter what form of schooling students may pursue as they grow up and even when a person is an adult, assignments need to be completed for classes.

When you are an adult and when you have a job, you may wish to further your education so that you can be happier at work and have more money for essentials and for the niceties of life; however, what is even more important is that you have quality time with your family and friends who enjoy your company and who need you. Also, while having the desire to advance can be very compelling, you are complemented by your family and by your friends.

Advancement is always a great goal to have, although we all know that life is short. Let's take some realistic examples.

If you are a parent, your significant other and your children enjoy the results of your employment, such as their clothes, their food, their technological devices, and the house or the apartment that all of you live in. Nevertheless, if you devote so much time to your work and to your studies, there is the tendency to overlook the quality of life between all of you.

If you have an elderly parent and if you are working and studying all of the time, we all know that accidents and natural deaths do unfortunately occur.

In other words, moderation is the key ingredient in having a balance between your personal life and your professional life. Indeed, you can have the best of both worlds so that you are personally happy, so that your family is happy, so that your friends are happy, and so that your bosses are happy with the quality of your work.

With all of this being considered, your purpose for wishing to have an educational life needs to be addressed. You do have the right to enjoy learning. You do have the right to feel fulfilled by what you can learn.

Even if you have earned an advanced degree, weren't there any courses that you wanted to take, but you weren't able to fit them into your curriculum due to the need to fulfill your major and possibly your minor?

There is another aspect of an advanced educational life to consider. If you are single, you can meet new people in your classes. You can learn and work with other people. In turn, if you have the desire to date, you are opening the opportunities of more relationships. Of course, that should not be your primary goal. If it is your primary goal, please also consider other ways to include more people in your life, such as social networks and mutual friends.

Another worthy consideration of an advanced educational life is that if you are in a relationship or if you have a family, you can become that much more informed. The direct result will be that you will earn that much more respect from others, when and if you wish to share your new knowledge from what you have learned.

If you wish to advance in knowledge and as far as possible in salary, you most certainly do deserve the right to fulfill this goal. Education can ultimately permit you to fulfill this dream.

If you wish to become a more learned individual, congratulations for wanting to do this. The next decision to make is where to attend school. You may wish to check out local adult school programs, community center programs, vocational schools, colleges, and universities, if you prefer to attend a specific environment for learning. Should time and where you live be factors, you might want to consider online classes. Again, it all depends on what kind of schedule you have, when to pursue more education, when such classes are offered, and the cost of tuition, books, and any other supplies that are needed.

If you are planning to earn a degree for your job, it is best to check all of the required classes to take and to formulate an action plan for how many classes you realistically can take each semester or quarter.

You then can devise a schedule of your classes for the completion of a series of classes and/or a degree.

If you are taking classes just for fun, there is no need for determining a time plan. Under these circumstances, you may want to immerse yourself in only one class per grading period. The benefit of doing so is that you can concentrate all of your efforts on the one class without imposing any additional stress upon yourself with other classes as well. Thus, you will also be able to enjoy each class each grading period without overburdening yourself with assignments that can result in a lot of time and effort.

Additionally, you may already have enough responsibilities along with taking the one class, and it will provide you an escape, to enjoy this "scheduled vacation" weekly from your normal obligations, if you will.

Along with accepting your craving to achieve a more fruitful educational life, you may feel that there are still other barriers to overcome. You may be thinking of any or all of the following:

1. How can I go to school? I don't have any time.
2. How will I be able to afford attending school?
3. Even if I do go to school, I don't want to fail.
4. What if I don't understand the material and I fail?
5. I don't want anyone to think I am dumb, especially the teachers and the other students.

Let's take the above concerns and shed some light on each with the ultimate goal to relieve these stressors.

The first question deals with how you can possibly attend school due to the fact that you may not have sufficient time. Granted, you do have responsibilities—to maintain your dwellings, to take care of the family if you have a family—and you do want to enjoy the fruits of your labor. These are realistic basics that need to be maintained and deserve time, attention, and energy.

Nevertheless, while all of the above will always be very important, so are you. What are you doing in order to fulfill your own desires and needs? How do you balance a life of responsibilities with your life to be self-full? While it is easier said than done, you need to make time for yourself so that you will feel full emotionally and academically and so that you do not resent not having the opportunity to do what you want.

A very good comparison is the need to exercise. If you exercise, you are helping yourself physically. If you do not put in the time to exercise, this may result in health issues. So, taking care of yourself truly is a necessity.

To reach your goal of self-fulfillment, it may mean ordering your priorities, as was explained in an earlier chapter. Above all else, please remember that you do not need anyone's permission to fulfill your own dreams. This is crucial for you to understand! You deserve to enjoy your life filled with learning and creativity.

In terms of the second question, about the expense of taking a class, if you have some savings, that may be helpful. If you do not have access to extra savings, perhaps the school or college you plan on attending has a loan, a grant, or a scholarship available. You could check with a school official, like a counselor or another administrator, for possible funding. You may also want to research online for the college or the school's possible loans, grants, or scholarships that you could apply for. A website like Scholarships.com (https://www.scholarships.com), along with many other Google searches for scholarships, can be rather beneficial.

No matter how you wish to obtain additional money, it is a good idea to find out if you qualify. Also, the sooner that you apply, the better. It is always a good idea to make sure you submit your scholarship application in full before the deadline, seeing that they will not accept late applicants.

Upon gaining enough funds to further your education, please be sure to get enough paper, pencils, pens, binders, notebooks, and any other supplies for your class. You may be able to find out what you specifically need on the teacher's website or from the course catalog. Otherwise, you will need to wait for the first day of class.

In preparation for your class, please be sure to order the required books in advance. You may be able to find out what textbooks you need from either the college or school bookstore or from the college or school's website. One very good website that enables you to compare and contrast textbook costs at different bookstores is http://www.isbn.nu. On this particular website, you can provide the words in the title, the author, the subject, or the ISBN.

Please be sure that the textbook you search for is exactly the same one that is required for the class. In other words, if you are required to have a 2018 textbook, a 2017 textbook is not the right one. It may have been updated by the textbook company. Also, the ISBN is exceptionally important, as the number needs to be the same one for your class. Even if it is off by one number, it may be the wrong version. Of course, if the teacher gives you the option of several years or ISBNs, that is fine.

If you wish to rent textbooks, this is a very good option so that you can return them to the appropriate company upon completion of each class. Of course, please be sure to keep them in good condition so that you are not stuck paying for damages of any kind.

If you prefer to have the paper textbooks, so be it. That is your preference.

If you know of anyone who has taken the class and is willing to let you borrow the textbook, fine. This is a great way to save money. In this case, out of respect to the person who lets you borrow it, returning it after using it is important to do, and you may even wish to present him or her a small gift as a way to express your gratitude.

Another possibility that probably will be less expensive is to purchase e-books. This means that you can download the content onto a technological device, such as a smartphone or a tablet. In this way, you will have to transport only this device instead of any number of books.

Oftentimes, professors will have developed their own textbooks that can only be purchased at the bookstore or through the school or college's website. In that case, if you know of anyone who has taken the class and is willing to let you borrow the book as described above, this is another great way to have it.

Before actually setting foot into the classroom, studying the first two chapters and taking notes at the same time can be a benefit in order to become aware of what is going to be taught. You will be able to feel a little more confident about what you will be studying.

It is always a good idea to quickly enroll so that you can assure yourself a spot in the class. If the class is full by the time you try to enroll, you can request to be on a waiting list or, if possible, go to the teacher the very first day of class to see if there are any openings. If there are no openings, you may wish to stand in the back of the class and wait until the next class session in order to see if there are any cancellations or no-shows.

After acquiring the appropriate materials and at your first class session, you may find yourself nervous and excited, all of which is totally understandable. This may be the very first class you have taken in a very long time. Please know that you do deserve to have fun learning about the world around you. In fact, your family will probably feel the same excitement and joy for you and from you, and they will truly support you.

By sitting in the class, you will find a new sense of openness to the educational world, a new vitality, and subsequently that much more self-confidence that you can enjoy learning. You can become that much more aware and that much more appreciative of this global society with all of its complexities.

Usually, the teacher will distribute a course syllabus dealing with the textbook, the materials needed, related websites, related apps, the manner in which grades will be determined, and oftentimes the schedule of quizzes, tests, and projects. It is to your advantage to review it in detail. If and when you do have any questions, it is then a good idea to ask the teacher for clarification. After all, your teachers were once students. Also, your questions always deserve answers.

The next question is about not wanting to fail. You may be placing a failing attitude into your mind that does not have to exist. When you are in class, you are learning by being receptive to the information that your teacher is conveying. He or she follows a certain sequence of learning, from the less challenging material to the more challenging material. When you focus on the learning and on the logic of the presented material, your side benefit will be the grade. No matter what grade is being earned, the information is much more important to be learned.

Nevertheless, if you are taking this class for a certain professional fulfillment, you may need to complete everything with a satisfactory grade or higher in order to earn your credits for possible salary advancement or to maintain your job status. Under these circumstances, it will be important to give the appropriate papers, including the course title showing successful completion, to your employer.

As far as not understanding the material being shared with you (question 4), again, you have the right to understand and thus to learn to the best of your ability. The teacher relates the information in the best ways possible. There is no need to compare and contrast yourself with others. The class is for your own enhancement of learning. The other students in the class want to learn the same information you are studying. If they knew the material already, they would not be attending the class.

Along with learning from the teacher, you of course will need to study outside the classroom. If you usually prefer to study by yourself, so be it. If you prefer to study in groups and to help each other, it is then best to make the acquaintance of fellow students so that all of you can learn to the best of your ability. If you wish to do this, please be sure that a majority of the time is devoted to learning. If it becomes more of a social gathering rather than a successful study group, it is to your advantage to respectfully and tactfully say that you prefer to study by yourself.

As for the process of learning, if you do remember some of the techniques for learning information that benefitted you the most in the past, you may want to consider them. If not, here are some other possibilities.

First, you may want to ask your teacher what is the best way to master the information being studied, if he or she does not give these study hints during the first couple of class sessions. He or she probably will have some good suggestions, like how he or she used to learn the information. There may be one or several websites and/or apps to consider using that may include additional activities, exercises, puzzles, and quizzes.

Another possibility is the following: You can take a piece of lined paper and fold it in half. You can open it up so that there is a crease in the middle. Then, write a question on the left side of the crease and the answer on the right side of the crease. If need be, you can use the back side of this paper as well. In this way, you are actually practicing writing the information, which may be better than just reading it, and you are using less paper, thus preserving the environment.

Upon completing the above preliminary step, please read the first question on the left side of the crease and guess what the answer is on the right side of the crease. Once you believe you have the right answer, then flip it over to see if you are right. If you are right, congratulations. If you are wrong, you know that you need to focus on that information more. Then proceed to the next question and the next answer on the next line and so forth.

Once you have mastered the left side of the paper, then see if you know what the questions are, like *Jeopardy*. While it may sound silly to do this, it actually can help you retain the information. Using such a method is good, because you can read these papers without relying upon your textbook all the time.

Another possible way to become knowledgeable about your class is to write down your subject's information on three-by-five cards. You can write down the questions on one side and the answers on the other side. The advantage of using this procedure is that once you have mastered certain pieces of the information written on them, you can place the known cards in a separate pile and focus on the other information yet to be memorized or that may still be creating difficulties.

The disadvantages are the following: First, a large quantity of three-by-five cards may seem expensive to purchase. Secondly, based on how much information needs to be mastered for your class, they are bulkier to transport and thus easier to lose, unless you use rubber bands around the stacks of cards.

One way to possibly save money while using the described method is to cut pieces of paper so that you can write down questions on one side and the answers on the other side. Then, you can use them like three-by-five cards.

If you like the concept of cards but prefer to use your technological device as your guide instead, a website like Quizlet (https://quizlet.com) will allow you to develop your own flash cards so that you can use them any time. Another possible solution is that since many textbook companies provide websites that correspond to the textbooks, there may be flash cards already developed for customer use along with videos and quizzes.

The last question listed is that you might think your teacher and fellow students will consider you to be dumb. Frankly, it does not matter what other people may think. You and the other students wish to take the class. You and the other students wish to learn the information. Your teacher is there to provide assistance in a friendly learning environment for all concerned.

As for the other students, they are entitled to think and say what they wish. If they present a holier-than-thou image by saying how smart they are and/or how easy the class is, let them be. They are unnecessary distractions that do not serve any purpose for you whatsoever. You are doing what you want, and their egos and their remarks definitely deserve your avoidance.

There may be times when you may be asked by your teacher to work in pairs or in groups. If requested, it is important to understand what the ultimate goal is. It will help all students to complete the assignment successfully and to learn the information. It is important to begin working together as quickly as possible so that the assignments can be done sooner than later. In turn, it is best to check with each other by phone, text, or email in order to make sure that everyone is remaining on task and is completing their segment of the assignment.

Online classes bring advantages in that you may be given the opportunity to go at your own pace without necessarily feeling any pressure. Otherwise, you may need to adhere to certain deadlines, although there may be some flexibility based on the online school and the teacher. There may be some occasions that you need to physically attend the class or meet with the teacher.

The teacher giving the online class usually will be available for your questions. In the event that you need his or her assistance, you will need to communicate with him or her by means of the way he or she prefers. When doing so, please be sure to be concise as to what your questions are. In this way, you will receive the precise answers that you wish so that you can continue learning.

Online classes can bring their own challenges, especially if you need more one-on-one attention or if you have a lot of questions. If the teacher and/or the school is in another city, state, or even country, that will mean finding out when to communicate with them. Your teacher may have many online students, thus requiring you to be patient for his or her availability.

Based on the number of students being taught, the teacher may take longer to correct work and to return it to you. When you do receive your corrected work back, and if and when you have questions, it will again necessitate extra time for any feedback. Of course, if the teacher uses online tests, you will be able to receive feedback quite quickly, and there may be explanations for any mistakes you may have made.

You may know one or several other students who are taking the same online class, which may be helpful in order to get another person's perspective and help. Although they may be in another city, state, or even country, they will still be reachable by phone, text, email, Skype, and/or FaceTime.

If there are not any other students with whom you can meet in your community, you may need to rely upon yourself, your text, and any other resources available, such as any websites, apps, and reference books.

While there are a lot of people who enjoy and thrive in the academic world, not everyone feels that way. There are many others who prefer to have specialized vocational training, and these people are also essential to our global society. Home builders, carpenters, plumbers, clothes makers, salespeople, and beauticians, for example, are essential for a well-rounded life. These individuals need to have thorough training in their fields and truly do deserve everyone's respect and understanding.

There are vocational schools that serve those interested individuals so that they may learn and perfect their skills so that they too will thrive professionally. In order to receive their training, the students need to determine where these schools are and when their special career courses are given. In turn, they can determine their own schedules and adjust them accordingly, if they actively wish to shift their career interests.

Another way to become that much more knowledgeable is by reading the newspaper, which allows you to judge for yourself what is being stated as being just or unjust, for example. It does not mean that you will have a completely unbiased account about all of the facts. It does necessitate getting a diverse set of newspapers to attain different viewpoints of the same issues, such as the economy and environmental concerns.

If there is a local newspaper that is considered to include extreme points of view (not within the realm of society's "usual" point of view), this too can be worth your attention and time in order to read and to understand different modes of thinking. When you hear varying points of view, you thus are able to determine for yourself what is relevant, what needs to be considered, and what needs to be disregarded.

Having dialogue with family, friends, and people you encounter in different parts of your city, your state, your nation, and in the world will allow you and others to understand the logic of how everyone thinks. When doing so, it is especially important to listen completely as to what is said. Then, asking questions can help you clarify what is being stated. Afterward, this is when everyone can exchange possibly similar and differing points of view.

It always needs to be understood that you have your points of view, and so will others. Oftentimes, everyone will concur. Nevertheless, there may be people who are rather adamant in their ways of thinking, which will result in no or little agreement. Under such circumstances, there needs to be a point that everyone agrees to disagree.

If they are your family, there needs to be a way to respectfully disagree without the issues becoming a major stumbling block for yourself and for your family. This author had a maternal grandmother that was of one political persuasion while the rest of the family was on the other side of the political spectrum. She would share her point of view in tactful, respectful ways while listening to the others. Thus, she was respected and loved in spite of her point of view.

If you have friends that believe differently from you, if your friendship is of more value than their differing points of view, please value the friendship more so. These are the times that you need to remember the reasons for being friends.

You can also learn about upcoming events that you might be interested in attending from newspapers, radio, TV, and social media. Events such as cultural fairs, art exhibits, and nature walks allow you to expand your mind so as to have a better appreciation of the people and the world around you.

Crossword puzzles, sudoku, and a variety of thinking game books and magazines truly can make you think in order to keep your mind occupied and informed. A very creative way to expand your mind and have fun with others is to either attend a murder-mystery dinner show or to buy such a game and invite others to your home to play it. These are great ways to stimulate your brain to think not only critically, but also creatively, so that you will be able to become that much more of an independent thinker.

Youngsters oftentimes have an untarnished outlook about their life, and they will have interesting viewpoints to understand. They oftentimes can give the most complex problem the simplest answer, which can be very refreshing. As people age and evolve based on their own education, attitudes, and experiences, their judgments can range from being totally accepting to totally unaccepting, which can create possible insight and possible disgust, respectively.

People of all ages, of all countries, of all religions, with various levels of intelligence, and of all persuasions deserve to be heard and to be respected. People of all ages, whether they are young or young at heart, have perspectives based on their own life experiences. People of all countries have viewpoints that can be not only inspiring, but also challenging to understand and may be good to adapt.

People of all religions can provide a multitude of philosophies that can enhance one's personal purpose of fulfilling one's own life. People with various levels of intelligence, from very little to a lot, can enlighten and expand one's knowledge and appreciation. People ranging from the very poor to the very rich, from the very conservative to the very liberal, can have educational value due to their perspectives. People of all kinds of sexual orientation can be a great way to view another's point of view about life and what happiness means.

Having healthy dialogues can illuminate all concerned. When and if clarifications are needed, there can be a totally new awareness and appreciation. New horizons of thinking can raise one's own consciousness, possibly instill a need to act, and create some sort of change, whether it be for one's own good and/or for the benefit of society.

Going to a library or a bookstore truly can be a gift of information and enlightenment. As varied as people are, there are so many interesting books for young people, for the young at heart, and for people who have "been around the block many a time." Books can be your gateway to a better appreciation of the world around you along with understanding different authors' points of view in the realms of fiction and nonfiction. Through books, there are literally countless hours of entertainment that can truly be your vacation without spending anything at all.

Nowadays, you don't even have to go to the library to get your books. Once you have a library card (which usually has to be acquired in person at the library), you can check out books, magazines, and videos online for a specific amount of time before they will be deleted from your technological device. In this way, you can save yourself time and gas, both being always nice. It is best to check with your library for this available option.

Conversing with people in bookstores and in cafés is definitely an education due to the diversity of people's perspectives about life and their opinions. In turn, you can develop new friends you may wish to see on a regular basis.

In order to promote critical thinking, there are two books for your consideration. The first book is geared toward adults and entitled *The*

Book of Questions, by Gregory Stock. It includes many hypothetical questions to inspire divergent forms of thinking. Readers are presented with situations in which there are no right or wrong answers, thus allowing people to analyze the situations to the best of their ability. If children are old and mature enough, they too can read it and gain that much more appreciation of how the family thinks.

The second book for your consideration is *The Kids' Book of Questions*, also by Gregory Stock. It is written for youngsters, although adults and their offspring both can benefit due to being able to hear each other's points of view.

These two books are extremely valuable. They can be used around the dining room table as well as on trips, for example. There are many interesting questions that can inspire thought. These questions can help people understand and respect one another that much more so.

While movies can be for pure entertainment or escapism, many of them can inspire and/or provoke thought and/or action, based on the writers and the directors involved. Besides going to movie theaters where the "normal" movies play, you may wish to consider going to see or renting independent (indie movies) and foreign movies. What makes these films so worthy of your consideration is that you will encounter diverse ways of viewing life that are not the mainstream and not necessarily always presented. While they are different from the customary movies that most people enjoy, there is a common sense of humanity to appreciate.

If you are interested in such unique movies, look online to see which ones may be playing in your area. There probably are not only explanations, but also trailers for your consideration. In turn, you can determine for yourself whether you wish to view these movies. In fact, it is suggested to sometimes consider those movies that seem rather not to your liking. Then, it is best to keep an open mind, because you may actually like them. After viewing them, if you view them with other people, this can be an ideal time to discuss those movies in order to see what all of you think in terms of what ideas are being expressed.

Television can contribute to your overall education, especially the educational channels as well as the news channels. In turn, you will be that much more informed about your surroundings. There are also many entertaining programs that can act as a relief from the trials and the tribulations of daily living. Of course, in this day and age of a multitude of channels, one truly does have many possible channels to select from, to enjoy, and to learn from.

Radio can be an enormously valuable experience for you. While music is important for one's listening pleasure, news about the world can be very informative. Another valuable part of this medium can be radio talk shows, whereby you can listen to people's different perspectives about life. They may be so inspirational that you may wish to act on this information—for instance, by working for a political campaign or for a charity.

The internet is an enormous fountain for your information, for your entertainment, and for purchases. Information on such websites as Wikipedia (https://www.wikipedia.org) and attained through such search engines as StartPage (https://www.startpage.com) are great due to the wealth of the information stored. In fact, there are plentiful websites provided for free and for purchase, based on what you may have heard about through the media, through friends, and through professionals.

Listening to stations locally and throughout the world truly can fulfill your desire to be informed and to be entertained. An interesting possibility is iHeart Radio (https://www.iheart.com), which is also available via an app. Another possibility is National Public Radio (https://www.npr.org), which provides analysis of the noteworthy events of the day, business, politics, health, science, technology, music, arts, and culture.

YouTube (https://www.youtube.com) will allow you to become aware of people's perspectives throughout the world and is also a great way to see movie trailers.

Should you have school-age children doing book reports, there are two websites for your consideration. Both BookRags (http://www.bookrags.com) and PinkMonkey (http://www.pinkmonkey.com) include many book summaries, analyses, themes, and related questions for purchase. Of course, reading the literature first should be done in order to fully appreciate its value.

There is a multitude of social networks worthy of consideration, such as Facebook (https://www.facebook.com), Twitter (https://twitter.com), and Tumblr (https://www.tumblr.com). These networks can provide many avenues to be in continuous contact with others and to reconnect with those you lost contact with over the years.

One major disadvantage of social media is that people can become emotional and will say anything, not realizing that others, whether they are family, friends, and/or professionals, may read and react negatively to such comments. One moment's anger can permeate to others who will not necessarily like this, and it may create problems either in the virtual world or in public.

In order to try to counteract misinterpretations in the virtual world, it is best to take a big, deep breath and to really think what the ramifications may be for people reading your posts. By doing so, you are apt to be much more rational in your posts. Accentuating the positive so that you are inspirational can have a resounding effect on you personally, helping you think more positively, as well as make you a role model for others by how you express yourself in the virtual world.

The other disadvantage can be lack of safety, due to the fact that there are unfortunately deceptive people who want to lure people for their negative purposes. While adults typically are more cautious, kids are much more receptive and sometimes gullible, and that can create problems for them.

If you are a parent, it is best to know everything that your children are doing on the internet, if and when they have access to it. If they object to monitoring, please discuss with them as if they were adults the reasons for your decision. It is hoped they will understand; however, if they continue to object, that is when it is important to be more assertive and to take any appropriate, fair measures in order to ensure their safety.

Two very positive tools for your consideration are Skype (https://www.skype.com) and FaceTime (see https://support.apple.com/en-us/HT204380) because they are a blend of technology and video communication. If you have a webcam or a smartphone with a camera, you can contact anyone else with the same features throughout the world. What is really nice about both of these tools is that they are free, aside from the cost of the technological device and internet access.

While you may wish to use this technology with family and friends, you can also link up with anyone throughout the world. It is important to know them or to know of them through other reputable people. In terms of actually talking and seeing them in other parts of the world, you will need to determine a mutually agreeable time to be online, due to the different time zones.

Museums truly are a wealth of timely events and creative people's work. For instance, art museums allow you to study at your leisure without any burden or stress of evaluation. You can visit as often as you wish. Even museums specializing in cartoons can depict different facets of life, oftentimes being satirical, worthy of thought, and worthy of discussion.

Museums oftentimes include docents that can inform visitors about different exhibits, give information about specific pictures, and answer your questions. There are museums in which you may purchase audio devices that you can carry from one exhibit to the next whereby you may find out information. There are oftentimes bookstores in museums, in the event you wish to have remembrances of your visit and/or to gain more insight into the different exhibits presented.

There may be certain days on which museums may be free to the public. Thus, you just need to be aware of such free days by going to their websites, reading about their free days in newspapers, and/or listening to advertisements on the radio or on television.

Other ways to broaden your intellectual horizon are by attending shows at planetariums and at aquariums, and by visiting zoos. Planetariums can most certainly be very informative and mind-expanding in terms of understanding what we do know and what we do not know about the universe along with questions that we will not be able to answer for many generations to come, if not longer.

Aquariums are a true joy to view and to appreciate the balance of your life with the natural world. You can become that much more aware of the need to preserve water, one of our many valuable resources.

Zoos are another fabulous way to appreciate the natural environment, because animals of various sizes are an enormous part of our world. They can provide an enriching education due to the fact that you can learn about their habitats and how human beings need to become more informed as to what to do in order to preserve our environment.

There are theme parks that can provide a wealth of entertainment for the entire family. Of course, rides are the main reason why people attend such parks. This is a good, fun way for people of all ages to be young at heart.

Food can truly provide a way to expand one's taste buds. Granted, with the expanse of fast food restaurants and children wishing to eat what they have to offer, it is oftentimes difficult to persuade them to try something unique. Nevertheless, with the parents' guidance, children can be introduced to foods that they are not accustomed to. In this way, the family can be introduced to a variety of different tastes throughout one's society and throughout the world.

There is also a physiological consequence to an educational life, because you are increasing not only your knowledge of the outside world, but also your brain cells, your brainpower to have an even healthier brain, thus again minimizing the chances of horrible diseases as dementia and Alzheimer's. When you frequently are introduced to something new, you become more enlightened. In turn, this can help you mentally. The last consequence will be that you are showing by your example to others that they too can become inspired. You truly can become others' role model.

KEY IDEAS TO REMEMBER

- Learning is an activity that requires a lot of time, a lot of effort, and a lot of practice.
- Many kinds of schools are available for the interests and the needs of the students; each kind offers both advantages and disadvantages.
- Education is continuous, even after you graduate.
- Moderation in working and studying is important in order to have a personal and a professional life.
- Wanting to attend school after having already graduated is good, and there are many options available.
- Being an adult student, either for fun or for work, in order to grow academically is good for your mind.
- Education is not limited to the classroom, but available in your local and global community.
- Many websites and apps provide ways to connect with others and to learn about the world.

8

ACCEPTANCE

Having one's talent or developing one's talent through inspiration and by learning can be very helpful and very inspirational. It truly can motivate an individual to become very innovative. On the other hand, the ability to be self-assured without being hypercritical and without taking others' criticism personally can be a challenge. This is why acceptance is crucial to understand and to internalize.

Before understanding the implications of the word *acceptance*, let's define it. According to the World Book Dictionary, acceptance is "the act of taking as true and satisfactory." That which is taken as being true and satisfactory allows people in general a state of comfort and relief so that they feel self-assured and accepted.

A positive belief is a norm that an individual may choose to live in peace and harmony so that life will be more fulfilling and filled with possibilities. On the other hand, if one believes that there can be no resolution to a problem, it is a form of acceptance or a form of resignation. It does not mean that it has to remain that way, unless it is decided to take some sort of action to remedy the situation. A person believing that he or she cannot change a particular person may decide that it is not even worth trying to convince the other person with logic, thereby just letting that person be.

One of the most challenging aspects of life is self-acceptance. You may wish to be a perfect model of a human being due to whatever your circumstances are and due to the people around you. When you have certain standards about yourself due to your parents or other factors from your childhood, you may decide this is fine.

For example, imagine that your family is large and that you are the oldest of your siblings. Your parents decide to make you become the in-house babysitter while they are out on a date. Thus, you are given the opportunity to have some control of your siblings by making sure that they complete their homework, that they complete their chores under your direction, and that they behave well.

Later on in your life, having adopted the habit of controlling people, you decide to become a manager at your business. It thus becomes easier for you to fit into this role of a manager as a result of accepting your role early on as that of a controller. You may also attempt to be this role of a manager in your personal life.

Let's look at another family situation in which you are the youngest of the siblings. Your oldest sibling has directed you during the early stages of your life, and it has been expected that you obey. You might have become so accustomed to being ordered around that you become complacent in this role.

On the other hand, being the youngest of the siblings and being told what to do, you may have reacted vehemently by rebelling, by using illegal drugs and by drinking alcohol, for example. The consequences of such actions could very easily lead to problems, such as addiction, some sort of confinement, and/or rehabilitation.

Later on in your life, you find someone who seems to be in good control of his or her life, and you feel comfortable for the rest of your life following that person's rules. Otherwise, you may again become rebellious and get married and divorced several times. In fact, you may rebel so much that you became a runaway or a criminal, because you hate being controlled by anyone. The fact of the matter is that with your being the youngest in the family and having to obey your oldest sibling, you have never had the opportunity to be accepted for who you are. Nobody listened to you. Nobody respected you. This is regrettable, to say the least.

Nevertheless, while you cannot do anything about how people treated you in the past, you and only you are responsible for how you behave and for how you want to be treated in the present. When you authentically practice tact and respect for others, you will then be accepted for the most part. Granted, it does take a lot of self-appraisal, courage, time, and patience with one's self in order to be self-respectful and respectful of others, but it can be worth it so that you can have a better life for yourself and with others.

There can be people who will go from not accepting themselves to the opposite extreme. They will feel they are entitled to everything due to their past circumstances. In a manner of speaking, this is a form of passive anger or rebellion against others around them that may or may not have caused them to doubt themselves.

Some people will almost demand that their beliefs are more important than others. In fact, everyone's beliefs are important to be recognized and respected, even if these beliefs are contradictory to our own. Of course, if these beliefs inflict pain or worse on others, immediate action needs to be taken, such as even possibly calling the police when and if it is bad enough.

If the innocent people did not create their past, when people who were hurt then hurt others, this will create many ill feelings. If the guilty people did create their past, intense counseling needs to take place to heal from the past, although this is easier said than done. Some guilty people may be in such denial that they cannot possibly confront their own mistakes and will rationalize all of their malicious behaviors, no matter how much the consequences are brought up to them.

It is thus important to learn how to compromise with others without demanding or hurting others in the process. Yes, compromise necessitates at least two people agreeing to come up with a solution so that each person's own needs are fulfilled to one degree or another, along with allowing the relationship to flourish. After all, life is truly short.

While there are a lot of people who will contend that we have lived before, we can rationalize all we want, but all we know right now is that today exists. Today's people are right here and now. We do not know if they are going to be with us in the next minute, in the next hour, in the next day, or in the next month. Indeed, seizing the day and relishing our own needs along with nourishing our relationships are exceedingly important. After all, we are social beings.

For those who wish to rationalize that their own needs take precedence over others in order to circumvent any kind of relationship, they are missing the point of why they are on Earth. We are here for one another in order to support, to help, and to love one another. We are here to respect each individual's needs as well. As to how to achieve this necessary balance, this is when dialogue and compromise play important roles.

When there are certain expectations that people impose upon you, it may be difficult or challenging to find acceptance within yourself. People will want you to behave in a certain manner. Thus, you may doubt yourself and believe others are right with you being wrong. You then impose certain standards of behaviors on yourself that you might not necessarily want or even like. This is mental abuse at the very least, which is not healthy for any kind of relationship.

Here is another example. You live in one area of your country. You rarely visit your parents, who live on the other side of the country, due to the distance, the time involved for traveling, the money involved to visit them, as well as your busy lifestyle. They view you as an adult in terms of your relationship with your immediate family with your own children. Yet, your parents have conditioned themselves to expect a certain amount of cooperation from you. It is definitely a challenge to counter this mindset that they have instilled within themselves and upon you.

So, it is a matter of choice on your part. If you feel comfortable in the role of how to behave and are cooperative, you yourself have accepted the situation as it is. If you choose to prefer to be treated as a separate adult with your own needs and your own wants, it is important to take the initiative and to assert yourself, when and if parents or anyone else wishes to impose their labels and their expectations on you. This assertiveness on your part can lead to more self-respect and to more respect for you from others, although this is not a guarantee, of course.

Another challenging aspect is the acceptance of others. You might have certain hopes about the people around you. You could subtly suggest something to someone else. You could feel comfortable asking for a modification of behavior, or you could feel extremely uncomfortable based on your request and based on how you might believe the other person is going to react.

If you know that the other person is not going to change no matter what, there is a major dilemma presented to you. Inwardly, you may have a major struggle to deal with, because you may want to say something to the other person. Nevertheless, this will appear as being confrontational. There may be hard feelings, or it may even result in a fight.

ACCEPTANCE

On the other hand, you may want to just bite your tongue and not say anything, tolerating the behaviors as best you can just to keep the peace.

Here's a concrete example. You work with a lot of employees, and most of them are compatible with you. Nevertheless, there is one individual who is consistently negative while you usually are very positive in nature. You could patiently listen and never say anything. You could refute everything that this individual is saying, thus possibly and ultimately leading to a verbal fight. You could ask for a transfer of jobs, if that would be possible. You could try your best to not see this individual.

There is no easy answer, but the answer could be within your own personality and with your coping skills. If you are a tolerant individual, you can just simply listen to what is being stated and allow that individual the opportunity to basically vent. If your tolerance level is such that you need to take some sort of action, it is important to think about your choices and possible consequences in order to make the best decision so that you preserve your precious self. Let's face it: that negative individual is that way, and rational talks probably will not convince him or her, especially if he or she is very stubborn.

How about thinking of yourself as a pedestrian walking down the street? It is a nice, leisurely stroll. Suddenly, you hear a dog barking at you quite loudly from behind a fence. The dog is the negative entity, and you have the choice of trying to calm the dog or continuing to walk. The dog does not understand and probably will not respond positively to your kindness. So, you need to be proactive and to make a decision to move on, because you probably will not convince the dog of your intentions.

The negative entity, the dog in this particular situation, is probably going to continue barking (due to an assortment of reasons) at everyone that it is not familiar with. It is not a reflection about you, because all you are trying to do is to enjoy your nice, leisurely walk.

The negative person with whom you have to associate is going to continue being negative and argumentative for any number of reasons, some of which may be totally skewed or biased. It is not a reflection about you. He or she probably will continue "barking," but it does not need to be heard or to be engaged by you.

You do have choices: to either remain wherever this negative activity is or to leave. If the latter is impossible and you need to be in that person's presence, although it is easier said than done, it is important to develop more of a tolerance or to gain the ability to "tune out" him or her the best way possible and to focus on your intended work.

As for the acceptance of one's circumstances, that may be more of a challenge. In this day and age, there may be times in which you may not feel exactly happy about not having enough money for many of the luxuries that you normally enjoy.

It can be more difficult to overcome any depressed feeling about not being able to fulfill your and/or your family's requests. At some point you may have to resign yourself to the fact that some sacrifices need to be made, such as not having those things that you would like to have.

This may appear unacceptable for all concerned, but it can be a way to accept the reality of your situation, and it can help you to set up your priorities in terms of what you really need and what you really want. Under these circumstances, it may help you to define, refine, and/or revise your financial planning for your regular commitments.

It also may be very helpful for any children you raise, since they will understand that "money does not grow on trees," and it can result in them becoming wise consumers in terms of their priorities now and in the future.

In today's world of reliance on technology, it seems as though it becomes much more natural to depend on our smartphones rather than interact with people; thus the art of conversation becomes almost foreign, if you will. In order to gain that much more confidence and be able to accept one's self and others more so, besides the already mentioned books by Gregory Stock, it is suggested to learn how to speak with confidence by working with Toastmasters (www.toastmasters.org). They guide you on how to interview and how to interact with others when you are evaluated for every word and every idea that you share.

No matter how others may perceive you, that which brings you happiness without imposing harm on others is what really counts. Your talent is one aspect of your life that can make you smile. It may or may not be of help to your profession and your advancement. If it does, congratulations. If it does not, at least you can learn from the experience. If it is a hobby that gives you satisfaction, it is then worth your

ACCEPTANCE

time and your effort and will complement your life along with your normal responsibilities.

KEY IDEAS TO REMEMBER

- Acceptance is "the act of taking as true and satisfactory or a belief."
- One of the most challenging aspects of life is self-acceptance, and that can have major repercussions.
- One's role as a sibling in the family can indoctrinate you to act accordingly later in life.
- Life is about doing one's best to find a balance and learning how to compromise.
- We are here for one another in order to support, to help, and to love one another.
- Acceptance of others can be challenging.
- Acceptance of one's circumstances may be a struggle.
- Programs such as Toastmasters can help you develop a confident speaking style.

9

BEING SELFISH VS. SELF-FULL

When a person is considered selfish, he or she may only want without any regard to others. Here's an example in Spanish literature for your consideration. Benito Pérez Galdós wrote many books, and one of them was a novel entitled *Torquemada en la hoguera* (*Torquemada in the Bonfire*). Torquemada was a very selfish person who owned an apartment house. He expected his tenants to pay the rent precisely on time and was not willing to be flexible. They would be evicted without any consideration for their circumstances. They would complain to him, but he never relented.

Torquemada absolutely loved his son Valentín, who was very well educated. Yet his son was extremely ill, and the doctor notified Torquemada that his son could possibly pass away. As any parent would react, Torquemada was shocked and scared about this possibility.

In turn, he went to his tenants to pray for his son, that he would recuperate. Then, he would allow them to stay in their apartments as long as they wished. Of course they agreed and were conscientious about praying every day. Nevertheless, Valentín succumbed to his illness. Along with grieving, Torquemada became very angry and decided to remove his unpaying tenants from his apartment building. Pérez Galdós emphasizes the point that when one has selfish intentions and is not truly giving for giving's sake, the result can be detrimental.

In our modern society, we have had the unfortunate experiences of knowing some infamous individuals who have been so selfish for their own personal gain that many people were hurt financially. They have been discovered, fortunately, but the many people who have been dramatically affected have gotten very little of their money back. Smooth-talking, greedy, and dishonest people have been the culprits. The ironic thing is that those very same individuals would not want to be deceived.

Besides these infamous individuals, there may be people you know in your personal and professional life who are very egotistical. They look at their own needs above everyone else on account of whatever issues they may have had. It is no justification whatsoever for being totally selfish. They may see something that is really nice and want to buy it. There is no concern about what the ramifications might be to others, like if there will be enough money for the rent or mortgage, or enough food for the month, if they buy a new car for themselves, for example.

These greedy individuals eventually learn the hard lessons in life, that they are a part of a community. If they are in a committed relationship, their partners will sooner or later become so frustrated and so angry that there may be a separation or a divorce. Also, if there are children involved, they will suffer due to the greed exhibited. Only then will the greedy persons realize that their only companion in life is money, that inanimate object that can bring material goods but not happiness, and that can quickly disappear.

Happiness is a luxury that cannot be bought. The only true happiness is developed with honest relationships with others in which there are compromises as to what can be spent and not.

Being self-full is allowing yourself the freedom to be yourself without harming or hurting others around you. You fulfill your own desires while still balancing the needs and the desires of the people who are dearest to you, like your family and your friends.

Here is an example to clarify the concept of being self-full. You have a great passion for watching a particular program on television. You wish to see it, if at all possible, when it is being broadcast. Your significant other reminds you that the two of you have plans to go to a friend's home for a birthday celebration.

If you were to be selfish, you would object, because you would wish to stay at home to watch your program. There probably would be a lot of negative feelings, like resentment, by others due to your being bound and determined to remain at home.

If you were to be self-full, you would realize the importance of this friend's birthday celebration and would want to attend. To fulfill your

BEING SELFISH VS. SELF-FULL

own particular desire to see your program, there would be three options available. First, you could record your program to view it later. Second, you could check on the television network's website to either view it or to read the summary of it. Lastly, you could wait for another time when it would be aired, like when there are repeats.

In terms of your talent that you wish to fulfill, it is best to reserve time for yourself along with considering your obligations to your family, to your friends, and to your job. It should also be noted that if and when there are people around you wishing to fulfill their own talents, they too deserve their time and their space in order to achieve what they desire.

KEY IDEAS TO REMEMBER

- Selfish people look at their own needs above everyone else on account of past issues they may have had.
- Happiness is a luxury that cannot be bought.
- Being self-full allows you to balance your needs and wants with those of the people dearest to you.
- If and when there are people around you wishing to fulfill their own talents, they too deserve their time and their space in order to achieve what they desire.

10

PRIDE AND THE ART OF HUMILITY

Before we deal with the topics of pride and the art of humility, let's deal with their definitions. According to the World Book Dictionary, pride is "a high opinion of one's own worth or possessions." Indeed, having pride for one's own accomplishments is very laudable and worthy of recognition.

According to the World Book Dictionary, humility is "meekness and modesty." Indeed, a humble person may have a lot of pride for what has been accomplished as well, but does not always outwardly express this enthusiasm in a very outspoken manner.

Let's deal with the consequences of pride. For example, you devote much time and much effort to a project and justifiably deserve to feel very proud of fulfilling a goal, especially when it culminates in being a personal and/or a professional success. You truly deserve to feel very happy.

People will congratulate you for your continuous efforts and your accomplishments. There may be celebrations, such as parties, depending upon the extent of the accomplishments and its subsequent successes. Indeed, it is a very positive time for you, possibly for your family, possibly for your friends, and possibly for the company that you work for, if it is work-related.

It is at this point and time that you can exhibit a lot of pride. If your ego is such that you thrive on attention for your successful accomplishments, you will not only want it, but also crave it. If someone ignores your work under these circumstances, you may feel really let down, and you may even decrease your performance for upcoming projects. You may have a very poor regard about this particular individual as a result. You may feel that he or she is jealous of you for having done that for which you have been recognized and rewarded.

There can be negative ramifications of such egotistical feelings and reactions. People will recognize your successful work; however, they will regard you as an individual who only gloats and has a very ostentatious attitude about everyone else. Saying you are better than others, constantly referring to your accomplishments, and exhibiting your product on your desk, for example, are the grounds on which you may isolate yourself from future work and/or have people not consider you for personal get-togethers after work.

Granted, you can justifiably still feel a lot of pride about your success, if you have completed this project by yourself. Nevertheless, you really don't need to boast about how good and how important you are. Being happy while being respectful of others is a fine balance that needs to be attained in order to be that much more successful while earning the respect of others.

When there are others that have contributed their ideas and their work into the achievement, it is important to recognize the fact that they were supportive and helpful. It is important to thank them by relating your gratitude to them directly. You may wish to thank them by giving them a gift in order to demonstrate the value of their collaboration in this successful project. If there is money involved due to your success, it is best to have already developed a legal contract so that everyone is financially rewarded. Of course, if there is a monetary loss, everyone needs to be financially liable and pay accordingly.

If you feel a lot of inner pride, in which you are not boasting but you are humble in your achievements, or if there are others who have helped you to get what you have earned, you are establishing a greater, better bond between yourself and others.

There can be very many positive ramifications of your humility. People will feel proud and happy for you. They will recognize the fact that you are genuinely very appreciative of the others around you for remembering that they collaborated with you. They will feel like you are an equal with them and not full of yourself or have "a big head." In future work, your current accomplishment will result in them wanting to work with you that much more, because you respect them as individuals as well as part of a team.

After earning such recognition, there is a tendency for people to want to do bigger and better things in order to improve the company, for example, along with earning personal and professional satisfaction.

It needs to be understood that there may be times of failures. These specific times can be regarded as setbacks, although one needs to be realistic that such things can and do happen. In fact, in a manner of speaking, failures can be good, because they make you more humble and more appreciative of the recognition you may have had previously. Failures are a confirmation that it does take a lot of work and a lot of time to possibly have success in whatever venture you pursue, that there are no guarantees even with a lot of work and a lot of time expended on projects.

KEY IDEAS TO REMEMBER

- Pride is "a high opinion of one's own worth or possessions."
- Humility is "meekness and modesty."
- There are positive and negative consequences for your success, based upon your attitude.
- Failures can be good, because they make you more humble and more appreciative of the recognition you may have had previously.

11

THE GRATITUDE ATTITUDE

Your life is filled with many responsibilities on a regular basis. You do your best to fulfill your obligations in a timely fashion, both personally and professionally, for a more enjoyable life.

Granted, there can be many major concerns or problems that are presented to you daily that may create stress. Some of these major concerns or problems can be controlled, and some of them may be so insurmountable that you have no ability to take care of these matters by yourself. It is important to recognize that there are things you can control, and there are things you cannot control. If it is within your power to make some changes either by yourself or with others, fine. If it is not possible, while it may be difficult to do, there needs to be a certain amount of acceptance to alleviate frustration and still be able to fulfill your daily and life goals.

Let's take a specific example. Families can be very accepting and very loving, or they can be filled with many disagreements and traumas. When family members enjoy each other's company, readily recognize and appreciate each other's value, and allow for each other's possible weaknesses, there is apt to be more harmony than any negativity. It can be a very positive experience.

When there are families whose lives are immersed in negativity, the last thing that anyone wishes to do is to gather for special occasions, like birthdays, weddings, anniversaries, during the holiday seasons, and, yes, even for sad events such as emergencies and funerals. While they might get together out of obligation, they will dread being in each other's presence.

Under these circumstances, some individuals will build up a certain amount of tolerance for those who are considered negative. It is hoped for the sanity of the entire family that some sort of reconciliation can be made, but there are no guarantees, of course. It depends on the depth of the issues involved and how long the issues have been taking place.

Here are some key ideas for your consideration for a more enjoyable life, provided that you are willing and not doing them already. In fact, it is extremely important to develop a good attitude for your own well-being and for your talent to flourish continuously.

Having the most appropriate mental attitude will reflect on you as well as the people around you. When your frame of mind is positive, you are bound to be more accepting and more realistic about your day. You will feel very active and energetic.

When you are negative from the moment you wake up, your attitude will be very noticeable to others who will only tolerate your presence, if not try to avoid being with you or working with you. You will feel less active and less energetic due to your mood.

In order to accentuate the positive in your life and thus to fulfill your talent and your creativity, it is suggested to purchase a book filled with inspirational quotes or to check the internet for daily quotes. In this way, you can have your daily inspiration and thus your positive attitude.

While journaling can be very important in order to vent and to cleanse one's frustrations, another possibility for a positive mindset is to write down all of the things that you are grateful for. Some ideas to consider are the following:

1. I am grateful to be alive.
2. I am grateful to be healthy.
3. I am grateful to have people whom I love around me.
4. I am grateful to be loved and to be respected.
5. I am grateful to have my family.
6. I am grateful to have my friends.
7. I am grateful to have a home, a condo, or an apartment.
8. I am grateful to have a job.
9. I am grateful to be able to enjoy nature.

10. I am grateful to enjoy my city or my town, and to be able to live in the country when time and money permit.
11. Due to being grateful, I have the opportunity to have joy for myself, for my family, for my friends, and quite possibly in my employment with my ability to nurture my talent.

Next, while having a positive attitude is essential, when you express your gratitude to somebody, it puts a smile on his or her face and is a positive reflection about you. When someone who does not even know you does a random act of kindness such as opening the door for you or pays you a compliment, your kind response for this gesture is generating a more positive environment for the both of you.

We are all a part of our society, and we are reliant on others oftentimes. If time permits and based on the circumstances, having a personal connection with employees can brighten their day. Just asking them how their day is going is a way to break down the barrier of customer and employee and allows the employees to be that much more respected as individuals.

Next, in order to uplift yourself as well as others, it might be a good idea to learn a joke, at least one for every week. The joke should be in good taste and should not be degrading to any particular person, group, or faction of society. If you yourself have done something comical and wish to share it with someone else so that you both have a good laugh, please feel free to do so. The idea is to lighten your life and for others to ease any tension that all of you may have.

Here is an example for your consideration. This author was very close to his aunt who lived far away, and her birthday was approaching. So I requested the relatives in that city not to mention that I was going to fly there in order to celebrate with the entire family, and everyone cooperated.

After having flown there, I was dressed with a black cap, dark glasses, no identifiable jewelry, a black vest, and chains around my neck. I also tried to disguise my voice. I even called the restaurant where all of the relatives were to mention to the hostess that an unusually dressed man would be entering, and that it was for a birthday surprise for my aunt.

Everything went very well. Adorned in the outfit and with the accent, I convinced her that I was someone else for a while, and she then said that I sounded like her nephew. That is when the others and I began to laugh. The rest of the evening was a great time had by all. Also, my aunt truly did appreciate the fact that I joined the rest of the relatives for this family reunion.

So, playing a joke on someone in a loving way like the above true occurrence or brightening someone's day with a joke is a great way to accentuate the positive aspects of life and to brighten others in the process. It truly is a win-win situation where everybody can laugh and remember that life is for living and enjoying.

While dealing with many different responsibilities, it is very easy to become so immersed in your work that you may very easily disregard the reasons for working in the first place. Granted, fulfilling your obligations of work can give you pleasure. Yet the ultimate purpose of working is not only to have conveniences like your home, food, and clothes, but also to enjoy the fruits of your labor, such as was mentioned about the five teachers from Spain who came to the United States to enjoy their lives in a different country.

Work allows you the freedom to do what you please within reason, to buy those special items you have always wanted and to buy that special gift for someone. Work allows you to have free time for whatever you please that is affordable in your budget. That may mean buying that special book, going to the movies, and playing a sport, for instance. That may mean being able to get away for the day. That may mean being able to travel out of town for a nice, long weekend. That may mean taking a long vacation to a place you really enjoy or to a place where you have never been.

Having a sense of gratitude or a sense of appreciation of what is available and what is possible in life is exceptionally important. In doing so, you can have a positive, realistic attitude that can be more accepting of situations and people without being condescending. You consequently are allowing your mind to open to devote time to your talent and to your creativity. By continuously doing so, a positive snowball effect takes place, in that many more possible ideas and many more personal and quite possibly professional rewards can take place.

KEY IDEAS TO REMEMBER

- Families can be very accepting or very negative of one another.
- Having a more enjoyable life will benefit your talent and your creativity.
- Your frame of mind will affect you and the others around you.
- Being inspired will result in a positive attitude.
- Journaling for a positive mindset can be very beneficial.
- Expressing your gratitude to someone can shine back onto you.
- Telling a joke once a week lightens people.
- Life is to enjoy the fruits of your labor.

12

OUR CHILDREN ARE OUR FUTURE!

There definitely can be a great deal of personal and professional satisfaction when you have accomplished your goals to the fullest. Also, you truly are to be congratulated and to be commended for all of your efforts.

It is ironic that in our society, we tend not to focus so much on the positive. Here is an example for your consideration. There are many parents who will naturally expect their children to do well in school. While there are parents who recognize and praise efforts and achievements, there are also many parents who just naturally expect these results and will only make slight comments such as "That's nice" and "Keep up the good work" with no emotion, because it is standard for their offspring to be successful.

While parents may have other priorities and thus are distracted from their children's achievements, such continuous nonemotional recognitions can be detrimental to the psyches of these children. They indeed have devoted a lot of time and a lot of effort in order to achieve their goals. While you, the adult parent, may have been brought up in such an atmosphere of just accepting these successes, you have the ability to change your family's dynamics and thus your children's self-worth along with future generations.

When you find out about your children's successes with such things as grades and their achievements in competitions, it is best to consider the following. Giving them a pat on the back and giving them a compliment at the same time are great ways to reinforce positive behavior. If you wish to take it one step further, you may wish to consider giving them some sort of additional award, such as extra privileges or some sort of monetary award.

While you may think that such measures seem childish, consider this in another way: When you as the professional have accomplished something for your job, there can be any number of positive consequences. You could get a high-five, a smile from others, and a pat on the back. You could get some sort of monetary award. You could even get a free vacation somewhere.

Personally, while you may believe and state that you are "just doing your job," underneath this statement is a sense of accomplishment. You are actually glad that you are being recognized for your creativity and for your ability. It is an honor to have succeeded.

In the same way that you are personally affected by your accomplishments, your children are as well. In fact, they are impacted very positively by being acknowledged and rewarded in any way, because it will definitely stay with them, thus affecting their lives.

It always needs to be remembered that our children learn from what we as adults do and by what we say. One constructive, helpful act will result in our children believing, respecting, and trusting us and themselves that much more.

One destructive act, by saying something negative and acting out angrily, for example, can push children into believing that they have to be on guard as to what they say or do. If and when parents behave in a negative fashion, it is important (though easier said than done) for them to recognize the faults and to apologize sincerely to those who were affected. It is only in that way that the children will understand that parents are human, that they have their ups and their downs although in the long run, they are loving and supportive.

By showing one's humanity with strengths and with areas of improvement, children too can recognize the importance of accepting the condition of being human. They see that they can make mistakes and learn from them so that they can become better people.

While recognizing one's strengths and areas of improvement can help people feel better emotionally and help them interact better with others, there are others who still cope with issues that can keep them from fulfilling what they wish to do. Nevertheless, as was already mentioned, authors such as Gustavo Adolfo Bécquer from Spain and Edgar

Allan Poe from the United States used their frailties to explore their creativity and thus are very well known for their literature.

Of course, the majority of people do not convey their thoughts into literature that is widely read. They do the best they can. When adults have children, parents will do the best they can by setting guidelines, encouraging when needed, and praising when warranted. Such behaviors can help set positive patterns and can be very inspirational for their children's lives in the future.

Our children are our future! Instead of being weighed down with family issues and the many demands of their education, they deserve to be inspired by the young and the old alike. Indeed, parents, teachers, coaches, and other adult role models truly do have significant roles in having high expectations sprinkled with reality, although it needs to be understood that our children deserve to have a quality of life with less stress, if we wish them to be happy instead of taking out their aggressions and frustrations on others.

It is hoped that you have gained more insight into how to create a fulfilled life for yourself and for the benefit of others with whom you live and with whom you associate outside the home. Having a more fulfilled life can be attained with the help of supporting your own talent and creativity, learning from others and helping others to learn, and respecting and honoring your community. All of these actions can be very helpful to not only continue your success, but also to inspire new thoughts and new ways of living for your own sake and for the sake of future generations.

KEY IDEAS TO REMEMBER

- Personal and professional satisfaction is great when you have accomplished your goals.
- Your success and your children's success deserve authentic recognition.
- Child learn to accept the realities of being human when adults model strength and self-improvement.
- Our children are our future!

BIBLIOGRAPHY

BOOKS

Brewer, Robert Lee. *Writer's Market 2018*. Blue Ash, OH: F + W Media, 2017.
Bryne, Rhonda. *The Secret*. New York: Atria Books, 2006.
Cameron, Julia. *The Artist's Way*. New York: Penguin, 2011.
Dickens, Charles. *Hunted Down*. Seattle: CreateSpace, 2015. First published in 1859.
Donne, John. *No Man Is an Island*. New York: Random House, 1970.
Galdós, Benito Pérez. *Torquemada en la hoguera*. Barcelona: Linkgua, 2014.
Gelb, Michael. *How to Think Like Leonardo da Vinci*. New York: Random House, 2000.
Gracián, Baltasar. *El Criticón*. (Spanish ed.) Seattle: Amazon Digital Services, 2011.
Ortega y Gasset, José. *The Revolt of the Masses*. New York: Norton, 1994.
Poe, Edgar Allan. *The Complete Tales and Poems of Edgar Allan Poe*. Lyndhurst, NJ: Barnes and Noble.
Reeve, Christopher. *Nothing Is Impossible*. New York: Random House, 2002.
Stock, Gregory. *The Book of Questions*. New York: Workman, 1987.
———. *The Kids' Book of Questions*. New York: Workman, 2004.

MOVIES

Braeden, Eric, and Susan Clark. *Colossus, The Forbin Project*. Directed by Joseph Sargent. Hollywood, CA: Universal, 1970. DVD.
Garland, Judy, and Frank Morgan. *The Wizard Of Oz*. Directed by Victor Fleming. Burbank, CA: Warner, 1939. DVD.
Margaret, Ann, and Oliver Reed. *Tommy*. Directed by Ken Russell. Los Angeles: Sony, 1975. DVD.
Phoenix, Joaquin, and Scarlett Johansson. *Her*. Directed by Spike Jonze. Burbank, CA: Warner, 2014. DVD.
Rush, Geoffrey, and Armin Mueller. *Shine*. Directed by Scott Hicks. Burbank, CA: Warner, 1996. DVD.
Spacey, Kevin, and Helen Hunt. *Pay It Forward*. Directed by Mimi Leder. Burbank, CA: Warner, 2000. DVD.

WEBSITES

American Bar Association, https://www.americanbar.org BookRags, http://www.bookrags.com
Chicago Manual of Style, http://www.chicagomanualofstyle.org
Facebook, https://www.facebook.com
FaceTime, https://support.apple.com/en-us/HT204380
Famous Women Inventors, http://www.women-inventors.com
iHeart Radio, https://www.iheart.com
InventHelp, https://inventhelp.com
ISBN.nu, https://isbn.nu
iTools, http://itools.com
Jeopardy, https://www.jeopardy.com
Kickstarter, https://www.kickstarter.com
Myofascial Release Therapy, https://www.myofascialrelease.com
National Public Radio, https://www.npr.org
NIA Technique, Inc., https://nianow.com
PinkMonkey, http://www.pinkmonkey.com
Preditors and Editors, http://pred-ed.com
Quizlet, https://quizlet.com
Scholarships.com, https://www.scholarships.com
Skype, https://www.skype.com
StartPage, https://www.startpage.com
Toastmasters, http://www.toastmasters.org
Twitter, https://twitter.com
Tumblr, https://www.tumblr.com
United States Patent and Trademark Office, https://www.uspto.gov
Wikipedia, https://www.wikipedia.org
Wyzant, https://www.wyzant.com
YouTube, https://www.youtube.com

ABOUT THE AUTHOR

Steve Sonntag has been a mentor, a teacher, his district's high school teacher of the year, a language chairperson, a tutor, a workshop presenter, a participant in high school accreditations, and an author over the past forty-eight years. He emphasizes insight, hope, and inspiration to students, families, and teachers.

www.ingramcontent.com/pod-product-compliance
Lightning Source LLC
Chambersburg PA
CBHW030144240426
43672CB00005B/259